I0469573

Jiggered

The Healthcare Insurance Industry; Unraveled, Explained and Exposed

A Handbook For The American Healthcare Consumer, Or Why You Don't Want Obamacare

C. E. Nash

iUniverse, Inc.
New York Bloomington

Jiggered
The Healthcare Insurance Industry; Unraveled, Explained and Exposed

iUniverse books may be ordered through booksellers or by contacting:

iUniverse
1663 Liberty Drive
Bloomington, IN 47403
www.iuniverse.com
1-800-Authors (1-800-288-4677)

ISBN: 978-1-4502-5635-3 (pbk)
ISBN: 978-1-4502-5636-0 (cloth)
ISBN: 978-1-4502-5637-7 (ebk)

Library of Congress Control Number: 2010913329

Printed in the United States of America

iUniverse rev. date: 9/21/10

1. Jigger - to interfere with.
2. Jiggered - manipulated or altered, esp. in order to get something done illegally or unethically

Dedication:

This book was written for you; the hard working, taxpaying citizens of the United States of America. You epitomize everything that's good, desirable and special about this wonderful country. You deserve the truth.

Preface:

This isn't a wildly exciting book. It's not a 350 page great American novel but it does have its compelling moments. It addresses the on-going controversy over the passage of Obamacare legislation and how it affects the relationship between healthcare providers and patients within the complicated structure of the insurance industry. It gives a detailed explanation of exactly how the healthcare systems and the insurance industries in this country operate and how that process will be changed with the advent of Obamacare. No matter what type of healthcare insurance coverage you have, this book will help you understand where you fit into the overall scheme of things, how your specific type of insurance works and how it will be affected in both quality and quantity over the next few years. You'll find that the only real crisis in healthcare is the one caused by the Federal government's inability to fiscally control and monitor itself. Federal programs are out of control. While there are many problems in the private insurance sector as well, those problems are far more easily correctable without a major overhaul of a well functioning industry. You should also be aware that this book is going to make you angry, so make certain you don't skip your blood pressure medication. If you pay attention to what's written here, you'll find yourself possessed of sufficient knowledge to skillfully navigate the pitfalls you're going to experience as a consumer in the insurance industry and as a patient in the healthcare system. You'll also find out who some of the good guys and bad guys are and how they're helping or hurting you, the American consumer.

In all the hoopla that surrounded the passage of Obamacare, the healthcare industry was eerily silent. At any moment, I was expecting providers to rise up as a group, as a unified voice to protest and set everyone straight about the horror that was about to take place in this country. It just didn't happen and I couldn't understand why. Why would the people most intimately involved in the healthcare system sit silently by the sidelines while their vocations were destroyed? Not until I sat down and gave it serious thought; not until I mentally dissected all of the elements that go into providing a healthcare product from start to finish, did I realized that very few healthcare providers have an intimate perspective of all aspects of healthcare.

Most healthcare providers simply do not have a clear and understandable point of presentation from which to launch an argument. They don't have the broad spectrum of personal insight and experience that it takes to present the subject in its entirety in a concise and well organized manner. The industry is simply too large and split up into too many different disciplines to allow most healthcare providers the clarity of view necessary to present a well informed, complete and concise overview of the subject. And then I realized that I should have understood this much sooner and spoken up to any and all who would listen. What makes my perspective unique? I'm a healthcare provider, a small business owner and I understand the money. I really, really, really understand the money. That's the key. It's an understanding of that money part that's relatively uncommon.

Very few healthcare providers handle their own billing. They use huge companies who specialize in the convoluted process of billing Medicare, Public Aid, private insurance and patients. Their payroll is handled by another company that specializes in the complexities of labor laws, employee benefits and State and Federal taxes. They have office managers who organize records and manage day to day activities for them and accountants who handle the intimate details of their finances; lawyers who handle collections and lawsuits. In fact, most healthcare providers have hired a complete array of specialists to handle all the complicated behind the scenes details of their businesses so they can get on with the process of providing healthcare. No single discipline in the healthcare industry has a thorough, in depth understanding of another. Healthcare is truly the sum of all of its parts and each of those parts is a separate complicated piece of the puzzle being handled by a specialist. It takes an expert to handle each of those segments efficiently. The expert in medical billing really doesn't know what the expert in payroll is doing. When it comes to the healthcare industry, the left hand truly doesn't know what the right hand is doing.

When I started out in healthcare and set up my own company I was blissfully ignorant of this complicated structure. I had a background in finance and accounting left over from a previous life, so in my naive ignorance, I firmly believed that I could provide healthcare and handle everything else as well. When it comes to money, I have always operated on the basic premise that no one would ever watch over my finances as diligently as I would myself. I look back now and wonder how in the world I managed it. It's incredibly complicated on a good day. However, through a perfect mix of naiveté, stubborn determination and an unwillingness to even think of admitting defeat, master it I did. It all came together as a complete package! Now, in another example of that same blissful ignorance I seem to be so abundantly possessed of, I'm going to write a nationwide best seller; right? So what if I've never written a book before. I've read scads of them. I should be able to do this because once again, I'm blissfully ignorant of the process.

Introduction:

Who is being jiggered? Who is being unethically manipulated for someone else's gain? It's probably you and everyone like you. You have a job, pay your taxes, feed, clothe, educate and insure your children, own a home or are saving for one and generally behave in a lawful, fiscally responsible and upstanding manner. You're an ordinary upper or middle class American. Some of you have made it through the daily struggle to realize your dreams and have found financial rewards and others of you are still working at it. You all have one thing in common. You're part of the solution, not part of the problem. Are you jiggered? You figure it out.

Make no mistake about it. The healthcare industry is business; big business; and many aspects of its daily, behind the scenes functions are dirty, corrupt and ugly. And yet, as a career it can be wonderfully uplifting and rewarding. Healthcare is not an inalienable right! Inalienable is defined as something which is impossible to take away; intangible and in the United States, when coupled with the word *rights*, is protected by law. Tangible objects such as goods or services are not described as inalienable and are not protected by law in the same sense. Traditionally, inalienable rights were defined in the Declaration of Independence and were comprised of life, liberty and the pursuit of happiness; all intangible. The key here is the word "rights". We can't walk out and purchase rights, stuff them in a plastic bag and carry them home with us. They're abstract ideals. Healthcare simply doesn't fit into that description. Healthcare is anything other than an abstract ideal.

Healthcare is a fee for service product which generates revenue and incurs costs on the part of providers as well as financial obligations on the part of consumers. No one should ever presume to think they have a right to consume a healthcare product without payment of any kind. Yet countless numbers of people in the United States believe it should be free; that the government should provide for their healthcare needs. And, in far too many cases, the government, through its entitlement programs does just that. But it isn't free folks! The government uses income tax revenues right out of the pockets of working upper and middle class Americans to provide "free" healthcare to millions of people who pay nothing for it; some of whom genuinely need assistance and many others who simply scam the system. When anyone consumes healthcare, they're consuming a product that has production and delivery costs. It isn't free.

Corruption in the industry extends from the government at the top and includes every aspect of healthcare all the way down to the consumer; yes, you down at the bottom of the healthcare food chain. We just witnessed a magnificent example of Government corruption with the passage of Obamacare. If an ordinary citizen engaged in similar arm twisting, coercion, payoffs and back door dirty deals like those we witnessed in congress, he or she would most likely end up doing prison time. But hey folks, that's just how it's done in Washington. Working, upper and middle class Americans are on the hook for Obamacare. You're already the sole source of support for the current healthcare system in America and you're about to experience ever increasing, in fact possibly devastating financial responsibilities in order to fund Obamacare. Look around! There isn't anyone else to support healthcare in this country. The Feds have no other source of income to support their healthcare agenda. If funding doesn't come from you, where will it come from? You have a whole new set of entitlement expenses to cover for the rest of this country. More than ever, you need to understand how this system works. Mr. Obama needs to redistribute your wealth. If you have more than your neighbor, you need to fork it over.

What about the rich? The government is going to take increasing amounts of money from the rich so you can have free healthcare; right? Well, the simple fact is that there aren't enough rich people out there to cover the cost of all the government sponsored entitlement programs functioning at the present time, let alone additional ones that we face with new Obamacare mandates. How are you going to find more rich people? You're not going to. They're becoming an endangered specie. Who ever decided we should penalize the rich anyway? How many of you reading this would like to be rich? I know I would love to be rich. I could buy new ambulances for my business and hire more people, buy a bigger building so my employees are not tripping all over each other, give out well deserved raises, and the list goes on. Never knock the rich. They employ you and pay your salaries. Take their money away and you lose jobs. Right now, most business owners are not willing to invest in any kind of business expansion. They don't dare. They have no idea what's coming down the line from the Feds. Every time they turn around, they're faced with new expenses to provide the tax masters in Washington with more funds to support a flagging economy. It's going to continue to spiral downward as long as business owners have more and more taxes piled upon them. With no relief in site, they'll remain in survival mode and unemployment will remain high.

What is rich? Mr. Obama thinks he can place a specific dollar amount on "rich". His numbers keep changing so its impossible to tell what he thinks rich is right at the moment. However, for the sake of argument, let's just say his threshold is $250,000.00 per year. If you earn more than that, you're rich enough to pay higher taxes. My company had a gross income of $2,500,000.00 last year. Am I rich? Should my taxes go up? After all my expenses, my corporate net profit was $1,306.00. Talk about cutting it close. The largest net profit my company ever realized was $65,000.00 and I can guarantee you, the government quickly snatched up its share. I didn't even have enough left over to buy a new ambulance which I desperately needed. Increase my taxes and I'm either out of business with 45 newly unemployed workers on the street or you'll have to pay even more money when I transport you in one of my ambulances. And to answer your next question, no I don't take money out of the company for my own personal use. I take a standard salary of $74,000.00 per year and pay my taxes through payroll deductions just like you. I consider the right to pursue, not necessarily to achieve wealth to be desirable; something I would like to achieve. I'm a year away from retirement age and still vigorously pursing that elusive thing called wealth. Somehow, I don't think that a landmark birthday will shut down that drive to pursue; that hope of success. Pursuit! Now that folks, is an inalienable right.

Who am I to tell you all of this; to lecture you? I'm an insider; an insider with a unique position in healthcare that gives me a complete view of exactly what's going on in the industry from the perspective of both healthcare provider and small business owner. More importantly, I'm an angry insider. Angry at what this country is doing to its perceived wealthy and working class citizens of which I am one. I am strictly middle class by birth, middle class in thought, initiative and perspective and I'm justifiably proud of it. It's middle class initiative that keeps the productive wheels of this country turning. Those wheels are slowing down. If the Feds are not very careful those wheels may become mired and bogged down in the debris of Obamacare.

Being in the healthcare industry has many rewards and benefits. It provides personal satisfaction and reasonably decent financial rewards. Even in poor economic times, there are usually still some jobs to be had. Most people who enter into the system as caregivers are not solely motivated by financial gain. They have a genuine interest in some facet of healthcare and in the human condition in general. If they achieve reasonable financial security, that's a good thing.

Many healthcare providers believe that the healthcare industry is economically bulletproof. In the past, that was true to a certain extent. Even in the worst of times, there are always sick people to take care of. Now, that remains to be seen. If providers are unable to cover the cost of providing services, those services will become very scarce indeed. By and large, the people who are providing your healthcare are not your financial enemy. Yes, that's who you get your bills from, but they're only the messengers. Providing your healthcare is unbelievably expensive, yet less than half of you are covering the cost to provide healthcare for the entire nation. Your President, with the help of his majority congress has decided who's going to get healthcare and how much of it they can have. However, he hasn't told you the truth yet about who's going to pay for it. Washington has many of you convinced that it's not going to affect you. That you're actually going to benefit. I'm about to correct that minor little misconception.

If you're a member of upper or middle class working America, you need to read this book. You not only need to read this book, you need to do something about the inequities in the system. The very last thing you can possibly believe is that a pack of Washington bureaucrats has the solution. I will have done my part by empowering you with the ammunition to change what's happening. As they say, knowledge is power. Use it wisely; Use it peacefully; Use it fairly. Most of all, use it at election time. If you've never voted before, now's a great time to learn how to do it! Don't be shy about asking for help. I'd be willing to bet that anyone who currently votes on a regular basis will be more than happy to help you through the process.

You have only one shot at trying to overturn Obamacare legislation. Only one! It can only be accomplished if the voting public replaces the current congress with conservative or republican senators and representatives; first in the November 2010 midterm elections and again in 2012 during the next presidential election cycle. A 2010 conservative congress could refuse to fund Mr. Obama's agenda thereby stalling its implementation, and a 2012 conservative President and congress could then eliminate Obamacare in its entirety. Once undone, a realistic, comprehensive reform bill could be passed. If Obamacare is not stopped by 2012, it will become an irreversible law of the land and the destruction of the greatest healthcare system in the world will commence.

Index

Chapter 1

A Little Business; A little Background; A Big Reality Check.

Never forget the basic premise that wherever there's big money to be made, there will be big corruption to capitalize on the financial opportunity.

You may personally think that everyone should be entitled to healthcare because it's the humane thing to do. That might be fine in Utopia, but it doesn't work in the real world. While that's a laudable ambition, it is not a reality. You have a choice. You can have the best healthcare system in the world with some limits on access or you can have mediocre care available to nearly all. Limits are naturally imposed by the number of people available to provide the service. Is there a balance somewhere in between? Probably; I believe there is but it will never be achieved with politicians making the decisions.

Let's look at Washington and their recent healthcare reform bill. Healthcare reform is a misnomer. There is nothing wrong with the healthcare *provider* system in this country. The bill that passed in Washington DC was not about healthcare at all. It was about reforming the payment system. Its stated objective was to provide healthcare to forty-seven million more people. The current bill didn't even come close to achieving that goal. It did; however manage to increase the cost of what we already have at the expense of the taxpaying public. Without going into specifics in the bill itself, just take a look at who actually decided the healthcare fate of our nation. Given the basic premise that healthcare is a business, we should look at the background experience of our senators and representatives. Only a very small number of our congressmen (and congresswomen) actually have some experience in the healthcare industry. Those same representatives had virtually no voice in the legislative process. If you're going to completely overturn an industry, wouldn't it make sense to have a thorough understanding of its workings? The vast majority of the decision makers who were involved in this process in Washington DC have no business experience, no medical or healthcare experience and have been in the netherworld of politics for years; some for decades. Many are wealthy and have probably never held down a hardworking, honest job in their lives. Talk about a disconnect from reality! And they're making our decisions for us! No wonder we're in such a mess. It's said that the best cure for liberalism is to start up your own business. You'll most likely turn into a conservative overnight. Perhaps Nancy and Harry should give it a try.

Most people think of healthcare providers as their doctors and their hospitals. Hospitals have a huge number of employees but they also have something else that most Americans overlook. They have a very large number of small business owners under contract to provide your care. That's right, a vast amount of your healthcare is being provided by small business owners. Your primary care physician is most likely a small business owner. Many physician groups set up private practices and provide services to hospitals under agreement or contract. They provide care from the emergency room to the surgical suite and everywhere in between. If these healthcare provider groups don't like their contract terms, they can and sometimes do, take their business elsewhere. That's why you periodically see a hospital change its service base. All of a sudden, your local hospital no longer provides OBGYN services, Pediatric Intensive Care services or Level I Trauma services. For whatever reason, the medical group was not able to negotiate a favorable contract with the hospital. Cost driven rationing? Most likely.

Those same small business healthcare providers also contract with Federal and State Government agencies to provide healthcare for

Medicare and Public Aid recipients, and agree to provide healthcare at a markedly reduced fee for their services. They provide medical care and then bill the appropriate government agencies for services rendered.

More and more healthcare providers are canceling their contracts with State and Federal agencies because reimbursement for those services has fallen far too low to cover the increasing costs of providing your medical care. Hear we go with rationing again. The Feds don't actually need to mandate rationing in order to cause it. They can achieve the same ends by simply manipulating production costs upward and forcing reimbursements downward. Then, when rationing occurs out of necessity due to scarcity, they can play innocent, blame the healthcare providers and insurance companies and cry foul when they're accused of creating a rationing atmosphere. I believe the political term the Feds would use here is unintended consequences. Do you think, for one minute that those consequences are either unexpected or unintended?

Healthcare providers and hospitals are in the middle of a very nasty squeeze. On one hand, they are facing ever escalating costs to provide your care and on the other hand, they are facing less and less income for the services that they render. During all of the heated debates over Obamacare, you never heard one word about trying to lower the costs that the healthcare providers incur in order to provide your care. In fact, you heard the exact opposite.

Manufacturers of medical devices are now about to be levied with a heavy tax on their products. These companies are, for the most part, large publicly traded corporations and are not about to eat the increased cost to produce their products. They need to make a profit to satisfy their shareholders. Manufacturers are going to pass that tax on to the healthcare providers who purchase and use those devices to provide your healthcare. That cost will be passed on to the patient population in the form of increased costs for pacemakers, wheelchairs, monitors, IV pumps and everything else you can think of. Countless increases in actual business expenses such as this one are forcing the cost of providing your healthcare through the ceiling. In this instance, the Feds just manipulated the cost to provide your healthcare upward. Where will the money come from to pay for these increases? The Feds know fully well that these costs will end up being passed on first to the healthcare providers and from there on to the consumers. You're going to have to pay or do without. If you follow the money, you will easily understand that the Federal government has every intention of placing such an overwhelming burden upon the private sector of the healthcare industry that it will rapidly collapse and they will then be able to seize control of another business "to big to fail" and completely socialize the system. There is no business "to big to fail" and that includes the Federal government. We have Greece to look to for an example.

Don't let any politician tell you that any monies will be saved under the "new" healthcare system known as Obamacare. It's just basic economics and Washington believes the American people are too stupid to understand how it all works. So now, I will give you a short introductory lesson in the basic principles of finance and economics.

It's common sense. If the cost of producing a product remains constant (or escalates) and you decide to increase its supply in the marketplace, you will have to increase your financial investment in your marketplace product. If you decrease the supply of any product the opposite will hold true. You will have decreased the cost of putting the product out into the marketplace by decreasing the amount you produced. However, when you decrease the amount of product you are making available in order to control your costs, you will be unable to meet all of the demand for the product. Therefore the cost to the consumer will rise due to scarcity and many consumers will go without. Many people who want your product will not be able to find it due to the limited supply available or afford it due to its expense. Supply and demand are the issues here. When a product is plentiful, costs fall due to availability and lack of competition. When a product is limited, costs rise due to scarcity. Healthcare is a product and has a limited supply; limited by the number of people who work in the industry. Under Obamacare, that product will become increasingly more difficult to find as the demand for the product increases.

The law of supply and demand is very easy to understand. It's completely logical. Let's apply that law to healthcare providers. If you suddenly place a large number of new healthcare providers into the marketplace and the number of patients remains reasonably constant, the healthcare providers will need to compete for your business by competitive pricing and high quality service. If the opposite happens and the supply of healthcare providers goes down but the number of patients remains about the same, some patients are not going to be able to find anyone to take care of them and the price for healthcare will most likely rise due to scarcity. Now let's look at what happens when the number of consumers (or patients) changes. If the number of healthcare providers stays the same and then there's an increase in the number of people who want healthcare, there won't be enough to go around. This is exactly what Obamacare is all about. Supply and demand are key elements of healthcare services that the Feds can and will manipulate to meet the needs of their own agenda. However, there's one major fatal flaw in the Feds plan. They can't provide healthcare to a large number of new consumers because they're not going to be able to increase the number of healthcare providers. That, at least for the time being, is not in their hands. They can; however, withhold reimbursement for medical procedures and care they deem wasteful. If granny needs a hip replacement and she's beyond the age the Feds decide to fund, she can't have that new hip The Feds are in absolute control over who gets funding for what care.

As you read through this book, ask yourself "is this a supply problem or a demand problem and who is controlling the distribution of our healthcare goods and services; the end product?" Watch out for *unintended* consequences and ask yourself if those consequences were really unintended at all. The Obama administration knows fully well that the cost to provide care for our elderly seniors is on the rise and will reach a fiscal crisis point sometime over the next two decades. This administration appears to be bent upon seeing to it that we don't waste our national wealth by providing too much care for this sector of our population. Limiting the type of healthcare services the government will approve for payment is an effective method of reducing costs. The Feds can, and will limit healthcare in the elderly population. They already do. Medicare does not cover anywhere near the amount or type of healthcare services that a private insurance company does. By limiting care to the elderly, the monies saved can then be redistributed to other patient populations deemed more worthy; an assessment based upon their probable future productivity and contribution to society.

The Obama administration has determined that we will be able to supply healthcare to several million additional people without increasing the cost of doing so and with no plan in place to increase the supply side of the equation; the healthcare providers. In fact, the administration would have us believe that we can increase the supply of the product with the same resources currently in play and save money at the same time. There's only one way there could be any reduction in the overall cost. Reduce the amount of money being paid to healthcare providers for Medicare and Public Aid services. That absolutely won't work. The further you reduce the amount of money paid to the providers for their services, the fewer providers you will have available to get the job done and the less product you will have to spread around to those who need it. If the providers are unable to cover their costs, they can't continue to produce their product; your healthcare services. They either quit altogether or they decrease their services and no longer provide care to Medicare and Public Aid recipients. That's already happening to a certain extent and will become epidemic with further decreases in reimbursements.

Every government supported entitlement healthcare program out there doesn't reimburse at the full cost of providing healthcare services with one exception; Federal employee insurance plans. Federal employees have it made and the American people are paying out of their tax dollars! They have one of the best private insurance plans available. Let's change that. Let's require that Federal employees pay for their own insurance just like the rest of working Americans and let's take a closer look at their retirement benefits while we're at it.

The results of continual under funding of our healthcare programs will be a rationed and corrupted product. We will need to spread a decreasing supply of available healthcare services to an increasing consumer base. Healthcare providers will spend less and less time with each of their patients in order to see more patients in the same allotment of time. The quality of that care will most certainly be corrupted. The only other way to cover costs and increase the available volume of providers is to tax the living hell out of you guys so that healthcare providers can afford to do their job; so the profession can attract or entice our young people into the profession. Here is an actual example of what happens in the real world of healthcare from a financial standpoint.

Let's say that my ambulance company transports a patient with private healthcare insurance over a long distance and the trip takes about four hours. We receive $3000.00 for our services from the insurance company. Then let's compare payment for that same service to the other major sources of reimbursement; Federally funded Medicare and Public Aid.

Private Insurance: *1 patient is equal to* *$3000.00* *4 hours*

Medicare Part B Insurance: *4 patients are equal to* *$3000.00* *16 hours*

Public Aid Insurance: *15 patients are equal to* *$3000.00* *60 hours*

Not only am I going to receive less money per transport for Medicare and Public Aid patients, I'm going to have to spend a great deal more money to increase the number of ambulances and crews to get the work done. If this was your company and you were selling widgets what would you do? I can tell you for certain, you would sell one widget to the guy who's going to pay you $3000.00, let the rest go wanting and have lots of free time left over to play golf. Healthcare providers are not going to expend huge sums of money in order to increase the supply side of their services for a whole lot less money. That's called the law of diminishing returns. Continuing to poor money into a product that brings in less and less net profit eventually leads to an upside down situation; the point where it takes more money to get the product to market than it can actually be sold for. When that happens, the supplier leaves the market place and the product disappears.

Think about this. When I purchase a new ambulance, no one in the Federal government is going to go out and tell the people who manufacture my ambulances that they must accept thirty five cents on the dollar and make due with it. That would be an invasion of the private business sector and would not be tolerated. Could my ambulance supplier stay in business if that happened? I don't think so. Healthcare providers are told exactly that when they render care to Medicare recipients. So, how do we stay in business? We get the funds to continue right out of the pockets of upper and middleclass working

Americans; those Americans who have private insurance policies. You are the only source capable of paying for healthcare and you are absorbing the reimbursement shortfall in federally funded programs. As long as the Feds can't pay their fair share for services, the financial burden will continue to rest with the privately insured patient population. By placing an additional burden of federally funded patients into the mix, the shortfall will continue to increase and the working American public will continue to see increases in the amount of monies they pay for insurance premiums and out of pocket expenses. The providers will have no choice. They'll bill more in order to meet that shortfall.

When the Obama administration addresses issues about unsustainable costs, they're talking about not being able to pay for Medicare and Public Aid at its current rate of consumption. So how do they propose to pay for the new influx of several million more patients, many of whom will be given government subsidized health care? They want to bring the costs to the Federal government down even further which means even less money being paid to the providers. Do you really think that's going to work? Welcome to the real world of Obamacare. Let's flood the market with demand, keep the available supply constant (or watch it decline) and reduce the amount that is paid for the service. Medicare and Public Aid are both government controlled and funded healthcare programs. So far, we know that Mr. Obama definitely wants to fund more Public Aid and less Medicare. Do you really want more of that? If your answer is yes, you want more government control; then you need to be prepared to pay a great deal more money into the system in the form of taxes. Be careful what you ask for. You just might get it.

We are not going to increase the supply of healthcare providers. Let's face reality here. The healthcare industry has nowhere near the attraction as a lifelong profession as it did even five years ago. The supply of healthcare providers will most likely decrease, if for no other reason than those who want to go into the profession will be faced with practicing in a substandard care atmosphere. Philosophical issues aside; the reality is those who wish to go into a healthcare profession will be faced with huge costs for education, killer hours of service, patient overloads and virtually no decent reimbursement for their efforts. Not to mention the fact that they are going to get their butts sued off every time they turn around. Get real out there! How many of you would go out and work for virtually nothing in a field with little financial reward after putting in efforts similar to those our young people undertake to become healthcare providers? You want to get top dollar for what you do and so do our physicians and healthcare providers. Healthcare simply isn't going to attract out best and brightest in the future because reimbursement will be sadly reduced. If Mr. Obama is telling us the truth when he says we will save money, we will have to corrupt and ration the product. Make no mistake about it; no matter what anyone tells you to the contrary, healthcare providers themselves will ration care out of absolute necessity even if the Federal Government doesn't (which they surely will).

Prevention! It's really all going to come down to prevention; right? We can save huge amounts of money if we can get everyone out there to do everything in a healthy manner. The government, in its misguided wisdom seems to think this is possible. They are willing to pour vast amounts of money down the drain by investing in preventive medical practices, studies and subsidies. In fact, if we don't behave and do what the Feds want, they will simply tax and regulate us into submission. Put down that can of pop and bag of chips right this instant, reader! It's time to face a few facts.

America is a prosperous country. Even our poor look reasonably prosperous compared to the poverty that exists in third world countries. Most people (not all) who are considered poor in this country and who are receiving Public Aid assistance still have a roof over their heads, automobiles, cell phones, big screen TVs and computers and still have a little left over for the occasional treat. Not everyone, mind you; but a large number do have these things. Being able to run over to the nearest drive through for a quick greasy burger and fries is all part of the American experience; an evolved way of life. Availability! It's out there and we want it. We want it now; we want it often, and we want the Feds to mind their own business. We not only engage in daily dietary transgressions, we already know fully well that it's not good for us. The Feds don't need to tell us. Were going to do it anyway because it tastes good and it makes us feel good. And, quite frankly, we don't think it's any of the Feds business!

Vast numbers of Americans who have perfectly good healthcare insurance policies don't bother to get a physical; don't bother in any way to monitor their physical wellbeing. Its boring, time consuming and the doctor is going to tell them what they already know; you're too fat, you should stop smoking, go on a diet, get some exercise and reduce your stress. Like this is anything we don't already know? Many Americans are reactive to healthcare issues, not proactive. Only in a medical crisis will many enter into the healthcare system. When parents are holding down one and two jobs to make ends meet, they're going to put food on the table for their families that's quick and simple. When they're cash poor, it's going to be cheap. Unfortunately, whether or not it's healthy is going to be a down line consideration.

Obesity; Yep, we certainly are a nation of fat people! The next time you're out shopping take a good look around. But here's a news flash for you. No one got out of bed on their fifth birthday and thought ...Hmm...I think I want to be obese when I grow up. Obesity is all about availability, self control and a way of life. Pouring large sums of money into preventive programs just isn't going to change that. The federal government's only role in this area should be to **educate**. Forceful legislation with punitive taxation in order to alter someone's eating habits or other behavior is an invasion of our right to control our own destiny. Politicians beware! The more you try to regulate the day to day activities of the American people, the more they will dig their heels in and stubbornly defy the system.

For many people, one of the most expensive events in their lives is death itself. We can't stop death. It's the only predictable element we live with. The only thing we know for certain is that some day, it's going to happen. Sometimes it's a big, messy, expensive event. Sometimes it takes a long time with large medical costs involved before it's complete. The Federal government isn't going to control that. They want to. They want to make certain that we don't waste money over the event; most especially, Medicare funds. The American people simply will not blindly walk down the path of euthanasia because it's a fiscally prudent approach to what the Feds consider a major problem; the cost of dying. Are they looking for a final solution? This is not pre-World War II Germany and politicians should not be contemplating a regulatory solution to what they perceive to be a fiscal problem. The right to make decisions about our end of life care is ours alone to make. We have all the support and input we need from our doctors, friends and family, thank you very much. We don't need the assistance of the Federal government.

When I began my career in the healthcare industry, I was young, naive and full of a desire to help the suffering; full of compassion and idealism. Surprisingly enough, I still believe in those same things after more than 30 years in the system. However, those desires and beliefs are terribly battered, tarnished and altered by a brutal reality that we, in the healthcare industry experience on a daily basis. What is that reality? **It costs a lot of money to provide healthcare and you have to pay for it if we are going to stay in business**. That's right; it's Business with a capitol B. However, I'm going to put up with all of the really bad stuff in order to get to the good parts; the good things that we really can do for the sick and the dying. Therefore, those of you who consume the product must pay for it. Do I wish that every single living human being could have perfect healthcare? Of course I do; but I know that wishes rarely come true without a lot of hard work and a lot of expense. If you're not willing to make some sacrifices to get your wish, it's not going to come true. Those of you who are not willing to make sacrifices, put some skin in the game, may find yourselves left behind in the race toward the fulfillment of your wish for comprehensive healthcare reform. Everyone needs to put something into the system if they want to get anything back out.

Is the cost of healthcare spread around in an equitable manner? Absolutely not! Upper and middle class working Americans are the only real source of payment in the healthcare system. You have private insurance. You're stuck with an inequitable system if we can't come up with a plan to change it without ruining a wonderful product. Despite all of the problems inherent in the American healthcare system, I still firmly believe that it is the greatest in the world. If I didn't believe, didn't actually know that, I wouldn't still be working in healthcare and I certainly wouldn't have taken the time to write this book.

I spent the first ten years of my career working in a hospital setting where I honed my skills to the fullest extent in the emergency room and intensive care units. After that, I turned to the ambulance transport setting; transports that involved the most critically ill patients imaginable. I practiced my skills both on the ground and in the air. Everyone thinks of helicopters when they think of air transports, however, that's not what I did. Helicopters only travel about 50 or perhaps 100 miles at a stretch. I traveled all over the world in private Lear jet ambulances to gather up Americans who found themselves suddenly injured or severely ill in foreign countries. I had many opportunities to be involved in medical practices outside of the United States; therefore, when I tell you that American medicine is the best in the world, I know what I'm talking about. I was not a casual observer like Michael Moore trying to capitalize financially on a controversial issue. I wasn't making a movie. I was in the thick of healthcare reality. I also returned patients from the United States back to their home countries who had been treated, stabilized and needed to be transferred back into their own socialized medical systems. Most begged and pleaded to be allowed to continue with their recovery care here in America. My Canadian patients, after receiving care in the United States never wanted to go back to their own medical systems. There is no medical care in the world that can compare to that which America is able to provide. That's both a blessing and a curse. The blessing is obvious. Unfortunately, everyone wants to obtain American medical care and many people come to this country in need without any means of paying. We provide their care anyway. Many are not in the country legally and the financial burden rests with upper and middle class, tax paying citizens.

I recently received a text message that I'm sure many of my readers will recognize. For those of you who haven't seen it, here it is.

If you cross the North Korean border illegally you get 12 years hard labor...if you cross the Iranian border illegally you get detained indefinitely...cross the Afghan border you get shot...cross the Saudi border you will be jailed...cross the Chinese border you will never be heard from again...cross the Venezuelan border you will be branded a spy and your fate sealed...cross the Cuban border you will be thrown in prison to rot...however, cross the US border illegally you get a job, a drivers license, a social security card, welfare benefits, food stamps, credit cards, subsidized rent or a loan to by a new house, free education, free healthcare, the right to vote and all without speaking a word of English...think about it.

Not nice; however, to the point and very close to the truth. If we get many more tired, hungry, poor and oppressed who can't take care of themselves, we will become a nation of exactly that; tired, hungry, poor and oppressed. The very lifeblood of this country will be sucked away into nothingness. Somewhere there has to be a limit. Somewhere there is a compromise. Somewhere there has to be a reasonable humane solution. It's time we went to work on that solution.

If a man stands on a street corner and gives away free candy, a line will stretch all the way around the block and further. If he says he'll give it to you if you work for an hour, he may not have very many takers. Free is not necessarily a good thing. It definitely can and does affect motivation and will most certainly result in loss of productivity and there will always be significant abuse of the system.

Illegal; what is illegal? It's any activity which defies the law of the land. Most Americans try to avoid such activities in fear of the retribution which may ensue. Americans citizens don't have "get out of jail free" cards. However, if someone enters this country illegally and steals a social security number, they get to play their "get out of jail free" card and not much of anything will happen to them if they get caught. Why is that?

Who's paying for all of this? If you're reading this book, you're most likely part of the source of funding; unless, of course you're one of the roughly 50% of the households in this country who don't pay Federal taxes. You could care less. You don't have any skin in the game. And you're probably not reading this book anyway. If you're one of those people on the dole, your not going to care one bit; unless, of course, someone takes away some of your free stuff or requires that you actually work for it. Then you'll start screaming and protesting in order to get your free stuff back. Protest (peacefully) all you want; it's one of your inalienable rights. I may not respect your position or opinion, but I will respect your right to express it.

Chapter 2

Private Insurance Funding: I Have Insurance So Why Is My Healthcare So Expensive? Why Do I have To Pay The Balance That My Insurance Company Didn't Cover? I'm Frustrated, Angry and Don't Understand This Stuff!

This is a complicated subject which I'm going to do my level best to simplify in a clear and perhaps not always concise manner. In this chapter, I will try to explain just how private insurance company funding works. There's an insider language within the structure of the healthcare payment system which must be mastered in order for anyone to be able to understand at least every other word when attempting to get information about their insurance transactions, its payments or lack thereof as the case may be. There are tricky phrases and words in your insurance policies you need to look for and understand. They affect, and usually limit the amount of money that your insurance carrier will provide for various services.

One of the most important things you need to know is that your insurance provider's payments may not be honored everywhere. Just because you have a pay source; private insurance, Medicare or Public Aid, it doesn't mean that your healthcare provider will accept it. They can, and sometimes do tell you that they do not accept a specific third party pay source and that you will need to pay for your healthcare services out of your own pocket. In that event, you will then have to pay your medical bills up front, and then file a claim to your insurer on your own behalf in order to be reimbursed for your expenses. Many healthcare providers do not accept Medicare, Public Aid and certain private insurance reimbursements as a source of payment and notices are usually posted in their offices or places of business stating that fact. That number is on the rise. Healthcare services are part of the free market economy and as such, providers have some choices about how they conduct their business.

First of all, we need to take a look at the private insurance industry. They've really taken a beating lately. Frankly, some of them truly deserve it and I'm going to tell you exactly why and who they are in the fraud and abuse chapter of this book. Others, however, are simply doing what they do; conducting business transactions for profit. Remember, I told you right in the beginning that healthcare is a business. There's no point in engaging in any business if you have no hope of making enough money to cover your expenses, reinvest in your future and make at least a modest profit. When you evaluate profit, you should base your evaluation on the **percentage** of income left (net income) compared to the total income, after all expenses have been paid; not on the actual dollar amounts listed on balance sheets. Most people would not quibble over a 3 to 5 % profit margin for any company. If you're personally invested in a business, or purchased stock in one, you're certainly hopeful that your investment makes a much larger profit. Isn't that the case? Before you vilify insurance companies for their huge dollar amount profits, find out what **percentage** they have actually realized. Let's face it. If private insurance companies don't make some profit, they won't exist and your medical bills will go unpaid. We would end up a single payer system in this country. That would suit many people until they found out just how much their own healthcare would be negatively impacted. Healthcare providers would leave the system in droves and both quality and quantity would deteriorate. Before you decide that private insurance companies are the bad guys, you should be aware that they are far less likely to deny payments for medical care than are Medicare and Public Aid. My company bills all three systems and has had far more payment denials from Medicare and Public Aid to contend with than we've ever had from private insurance companies.

The average American with **private healthcare insurance** has absolutely no idea what he or she is paying for, what it does and does not cover and whether it's sufficient for their needs. That's an amazing fact given the amount of money they, or their employer will pay to their insurance company over the life of their policy. Let's say, for instance that you and your family have costs of $1500.00 per month for insurance premiums. Over three years; (the average life of an automobile loan) you will pay $54,000.00 to the insurance company for your policy. You would never dream of paying that much money for an automobile without doing a thorough job of slamming the doors, testing the windows, looking at the engine and kicking the tires. Don't you think you should be looking at the engine in your insurance policy before you buy it? Many Americans are in for a rude awakening when they actually have to use their policy benefits.

Exactly what is a policy? It's a **private** contract between you and your insurance company and it sets forth the terms under which the insurance company will cover your healthcare costs and exactly how much of your expenses it will pay. Your healthcare provider has no direct knowledge of the exact terms of your policy. There are nearly as many different policies available in the market place as there are drugs listed in the *Physicians Desk Reference* on your doctor's desk. It's your responsibility to understand your own policy.

All insurance policies have some terminology in common which you should understand. Perhaps the most poorly understood policy concepts are deductibles and copays. While most people understand the definition of the words, they are clueless when it comes to applying those words to their insurance policies. They're unclear about how to figure out the amount of money they'll need to pay out of pocket for their healthcare services before they get to a point of full reimbursement for covered medical expenses. The most common policies are PPOs or Preferred Provider Organizations. These policies have both deductibles and copays as well as lifetime maximums, covered benefits and reimbursements at usual and customary rates. When purchasing an insurance policy, you should remember that you get what you pay for and you shouldn't be surprised when you end up paying for some of your healthcare expenses. If you buy a Ford, it's going to perform like a Ford. If you buy a BMW, it's going to perform like a BMW. Don't expect to pay for a Ford insurance policy and have it perform like a BMW policy.

Let's say that you're about to purchased a healthcare insurance policy. The first thing to consider is the amount of money you'll have to pay out of pocket before your policy begins to pay for any portion of your healthcare. This is you're **deductible**. Your insurance agent tells you that with a $500.00 deductible, your monthly premium payment will be $1000.00. The look of horror on your face is enough to indicate to your agent that there is absolutely no way in the world you can afford that amount of money, so he tells you about other levels of deductible out of pocket payments that are available and how much each deductible level will decrease your monthly premium payments. You finally settle on a deductible of $3500.00 with monthly premium payments of $500.00. Remember, you'll have to pay the first $3500.00 of your medical expenses on your own and as a provider of healthcare, I will expect you to do exactly that. You went into this deal knowing that you were going to have upfront expenses. If you're fiscally prudent and put that money away in a savings account, you should be all right. If you spend it all on big screen TVs, laptop computers, expensive vacations, fancy cars, IPODs and IPADs, no one is going to be too terribly sympathetic to your sad tale of woe.

The next decision you face is what level of **copay** you're able to financially handle. After your deductible of $3500.00 has been reached, your copay, or your next level of out of pocket expenses kicks in. This is a split payment of your medical expenses with the insurer and it's at a level you choose. You will pay a percentage of the cost and your insurer will pay the remainder until your medical expenses reach a certain dollar amount. Your copay is usually an 80/20 split on the first $10,000.00 of medical expenses you incur **after your deductible has been satisfied**. That is to say, after you have paid the $3500.00 deductible, you will have to pick up 20% of the cost of your care on the **next** $10,000.00 of medical expenses you incur. 20% of $10,000.00 is equal to $2000.00. So now you know that you'll have a total out of pocket cost of $5500.00

($3500.00 deductible and $2000.00 copay). Both your deductible and copay must be satisfied on an **annual** basis. That means on January 1st of each year you must start all over. Many people choose much higher deductibles and copay percentages in order to keep the cost of their premium payments down. This is not a bad strategy as long as you clearly understand that your healthcare provider is going to expect payment during your deductible and copay phase and you should have resources set aside to do so or a plan in place to cover those expenses. If you choose a 60\40 copay on the first $20,000.00, your premiums will certainly go down; however, the amount of money you'll pay out of pocket increases dramatically. You'll pay 40% of the first $20,000.00 which is equal to $8000.00. A 60/40 copay on the first $20,000.00 with the same deductible would cost you an additional $6000.00 out of pocket each year ($8000.00 plus your $3500.00 deductible is equal to $11,500.00 out of pocket instead of $5500.00). You've got it now, right? All you need to do is get that deductible and copay money put away and you'll be golden. Not so fast. There are terms in your policy that you need to understand because they're going to cost additional money.

Lifetime maximum caps on medical expense payments are your next concern. Caps are very simple to understand yet commonly overlooked by the purchaser of an insurance policy as insignificant. The "cap" amount is the total amount of money your insurance company will pay for your medical care over the life of your policy. It's not an annual, renewable amount of money. If you have a lifetime maximum benefit payment cap of one million dollars you'll pay less for you policy than if you have a ten million dollar lifetime maximum cap. Simple! A million dollars is a lot of money and you should be just fine with that. That's not necessarily so. A one million dollar cap will disappear virtually overnight if you or someone covered under your policy has a catastrophic injury or illness. Once your cap has been reached in medical payments, you're on your own. All medical expense payments are going to come out of your own pocket until you no longer have anything left. You need to consider this part of your policy carefully. Give it some serious thought before you make your decision. This is a lifetime maximum, not an annual maximum. When you hit your maximum, there isn't much of anything else left except financial ruin and bankruptcy.

Covered benefits are those medical expenses which your policy covers. The operative word here is **covered**. Once again, all policies are not equal and it's those "not covered" expenses that catch you off guard. My company receives countless calls from patients telling us they don't understand why they have a bill. They have satisfied their deductible and copay requirements and their policy is now at the 100% payment level. They didn't understand the significance of the "covered expenses" qualifier when they purchased their policy. On a daily basis, we're faced with explaining to our patients that their insurance company paid for their ambulance, but didn't pay for a nurse, respiratory therapist and the additional equipment needed on board the ambulance. These types of expenses are routinely denied as "not covered" despite the fact that they're needed. The word "covered" limits many potentially necessary medical services. Examples of care that might not be covered are maternity and delivery expenses, suicide attempts, expenses for pre-existing conditions and a host of other specific medical issues. An example would be a policy that only covers an ambulance transport during an emergency; usually provided by your local fire department. That might sound just fine until you think about it for a bit. What if you become dependent upon dialysis three times a week and are too enfeebled to travel to the dialysis center in an automobile? You'll be stuck with the cost of private ambulance transport services to and from the dialysis center for each separate episode of care. Private ambulance companies are far pricier than local fire departments because they have no funding of any kind through Federal, State or local municipal government systems. Fire departments generally transfer only from the scene of an emergent event to the closest hospital. If you're initially taken to a hospital without cardiac surgeons on staff and need an open heart surgical procedure, you'll be transferred to a hospital with those specialized procedures available. A private ambulance carrier will handle your transport and it may require a full four person team with specially trained crews, nurses and respiratory therapists as well as highly specialized equipment not stocked on board ordinary ambulances. In fact, very few private ambulance services can afford the prohibitive costs to keep these kinds of teams and equipment available. The cost of such services may run anywhere from $2000.00 to $5000.00! Read your policy carefully and make sure you understand the impact of those "not covered" services. All insurance policies have some "not covered" expenses built into their contracts; however, be very careful that the policy you purchase is not overwhelmingly laden with them. You'll pay less for the policy in many cases, but have far more out of pocket expenses to cover.

"Usual and Customary" is a euphemism that many insurance companies (certainly not all) use to get away with paying whatever they please. A great deal of abuse and corruption is buried in this terminology. It would seem that such a term would indicate a composite average of costs used to determine what the rate of reimbursement for a given service should be, based on historical and demographic data. Nothing could be further from the truth. There are as many "usual and customary" fee schedules for payments in the insurance marketplace as there are insurance companies. Each insurer has come up with its own convoluted, difficult and complicated formula which no one could possibly understand and then uses the results to derive a monetary assignment for payments to your healthcare providers. Some insurance companies have banded together and use a not so independent pricing agency to artificially assign low reimbursement rates for medical procedures and supplies. This is illegal and commonly known as price fixing. Specific cases are covered in the fraud and abuse section of this book. No two "usual and customary" pay schedules actually seem to match. As a consumer, when you see that your healthcare provider has billed above the "usual and customary" amount your insurance company will cover, you are incensed over the price gouging practices of your healthcare provider. Hold on a minute. The first thing you should ask yourself is "did my healthcare provider perform services that were, in fact outside the scope of usual and customary?" Did you receive care that was more expensive to provide than the average cost of taking care of a given medical problem. For instance, when your daughter had to have ten stitches in the emergency room was it a simple sewing job on her forearm, or did she need a specialist to repair ligament and tendon damage. Was the cut on her face? Now we're talking about the need for a plastic surgeon. There is "usual and customary" and then there is necessary. They may be vastly different in their overall cost to provide, but have the same payment assignment.

Usual and customary is an average of all costs to provide a given service and is calculated based upon services from the cheapest to the most expensive. If you received services at the high end of the medical spectrum, you will end up paying the difference between the average cost and the high end cost. For instance, you have been given a gift certificate for $600.00 to buy a big screen TV (lucky you!). That's a decent **average** amount for such an item. When you finally decide exactly what you want to purchase, it has a price tag of $850.00. You decide to buy the more expensive model and pay the difference of $250.00. So goes usual and customary.

In all aspects and phases of healthcare, price fixing and corruption have been rampant, long standing, malignant problems. This corruption has been engaged in equally by insurers, providers and consumers. However, some limited justice is finally catching up with the insurers. Now we just have to work on the providers and consumers. I learned early on in business that there was one insurance company that could be trusted to set a fair payment fee schedule and reimburse equally across the board. That insurance company is Blue Cross Blue Shield of Illinois. Mind you, this is not an endorsement and they have no idea they just showed up in this book on the good guy side. I refer solely to the Illinois division of Blue Cross Blue Shield and payment of ambulance transport fees exclusively. We have no knowledge of any of their business practices in other areas of healthcare insurance. They don't pay everything at 100% of the billed rate in most cases. What they do however, is assign and pay a realistic "usual and customary" fee. You are most likely still going to have an unpaid balance you'll owe to your healthcare provider. There are other insurance companies who also operate in a similar fashion. Not all are blatantly corrupt; but watch out for **most** of the big ones.

In the private healthcare insurance industry, you have a choice of insurance plans provided by **HMOs, PPOs** and every other acronym in between. It's up to you to become informed and make an intelligent decision about the type of plan you most prefer and can afford. A word to the wise; if it looks too good to be true, then it probably is. If you are contemplating purchasing a plan that is neither an HMO nor PPO, it may have a name with any combination of alphabetic symbols too numerous to list. Check it out carefully. Search the internet. Ask the insurance agent what expenses it **doesn't** cover that a standard PPO policy does. If the agent hedges on the answer, you may not want to get involved with that insurance company. Some of these plans are so limited in coverage they barely resemble insurance at all and they may take more money from you in premiums than you'll ever see paid out in benefits.

HMOs are **Health Maintenance Organizations**. While they have some restrictions on which healthcare providers you may use to provide for your needs and where it can be performed, when an HMO pays, it pays well and leaves the patient with far fewer bills to pay than do most other types of insurance policies. However, make sure you understand exactly what's not going to be covered and what the rules are governing the use and payment of policy benefits. HMO's are required to pay for your care in an emergency regardless of who you use for a provider; however, each HMO has its own set of rules for payment of non-emergent situations. Some are really great and some are really bad. Make certain your HMO has a very large provider list.

PPOs, or **Preferred Provider Organizations** are by far and above the most common form of private insurance coverage in use today. There is a good deal more cost sharing involved in benefit assignments than with HMOs. The unfunded costs are typically paid by the patients with some "not covered" expenses being absorbed by the preferred providers. With PPO policies, the insurance company will always come out ahead leaving the providers and patients holding the proverbial bag. The theory is that everyone will take a small financial hit thereby lessening the financial burden on all concerned in the transaction. Sounds good; but it doesn't work out quite like that. The lion's share of the cost benefit goes, of course to the insurance company. The healthcare provider is next on the list to benefit and the patient comes in last. In many instances, the patient is sitting with large bills while the insurance company receives a substantial discount from the healthcare providers. PPO insurance policies are the largest source of corruption in the private insurance industry.

What is a **Preferred Provider**? All healthcare providers are not preferred providers. Preferred providers are, in effect often entering in a kickback arrangement with the insurance company and many healthcare providers consider this an unethical practice and will not engage in the activity. In some cases, this is at best a shady practice and in other cases completely above board, desirable and beneficial to all parties concerned; the patient, the healthcare provider and the insurance company. It simply depends upon which insurance company you are dealing with and to what extent that insurer is willing to compromise patient care and enter into dirty deals in order to maximize profits. Some insurance companies are really good guys, some are really bad guys and some are in between.

Insurance companies hire employees specifically to beat the bushes in search of healthcare providers they can entice into a PPO contract which is beneficial first and foremost to their own company. Obviously, there has to be a carrot dangling from the end of that stick or there wouldn't be any takers. Surprisingly enough, after the insurance company gets a reduced fee contract with the healthcare provider, the carrot may be a benefit to the patient next and to the healthcare provider last of all. However, the benefit to the patient is very limited and sometimes does not exist at all.

So, who gets what in a PPO transaction? If it's a straightforward negotiation, the healthcare provider will agree to accept a reduced rate of reimbursement; usually about 20% less for their services from the insurance carrier than they have billed. In return two things will happen. The patient will not have to pay for that 20% difference but is still held responsible for their deductible and copay amounts. That benefits the insurance company. Any non-covered expenses **may or may not** be written off. If the non-covered expenses are written off, this is a good deal for the patient. If they are not written off, this is not a remarkably good deal for either the patient or the provider. The theory is it helps keep the costs of insurance policy premiums down. This is a debatable benefit to the patient. The PPO healthcare providers get their bills paid very quickly; usually within two weeks of filing a claim, and those same claims are not held up for any medical review process. Being able to collect on claims rapidly is of great benefit in an industry where medical claims can be stalled and held up indefinitely; sometimes for a year or more. Cash flow is a big issue and an ongoing problem throughout the healthcare industry. The other benefit is that the healthcare provider is now listed as a PPO member for the insurance company which may increase the volume of the providers business. The larger the PPO network, the larger the number of potential patient subscribers the insurance company can attract into their insurance webs. On the surface, this does not appear to be such a bad deal and for many reliable insurance carriers, their providers and their patients, the system works with some benefit all the way around.

Unfortunately, some of the largest and most profitable insurance companies simply scam the patients and the healthcare providers. The only thing the patient doesn't have to pay is that 20% discount the insurance company talked the provider into forking over. Not only is the patient left to pay his deductible and copay, but he may also be left to pay non-covered expenses. Remember that term "Covered Benefits" earlier on in this chapter? Or, when the insurance company pays the healthcare providers claim, they kick out countless charges as non-covered expenses and the healthcare provider is forced to take a much larger financial hit than he was originally led to believe would be the case. Those non-covered expenses may well have to be paid by the patient. Much of the time, the only real winner is the insurance company who got that nifty discount up front. After many years in business, I've learned the only deal that's any good is going to be the one I make with my patients; a deal which discounts their balance and gives them interest free time payments. PPO's just aren't always what they're cracked up to be. There are a couple of truly hair raising stories in the "Fraud and Abuse" section of this book dealing with insurance companies and their PPO scams.

For all the damage that insurance companies can and sometimes do, there are many who are reasonable, above board and reliable. Don't vilify them all. Right now, the only thing that's really supporting the healthcare industry is private healthcare insurance companies and the patients who own their policies. Put those companies out of business and you'll shut down the entire healthcare system. Why? Because they're the only realistic source of income that healthcare providers can depend upon. The private healthcare insurance industry is the only prop holding up the system. Pull that prop out, and your healthcare will disappear. Federal programs are broke, don't pay enough to cover the costs of services and are rife with corruption; far more so than the private sector. Medicare is in a real mess and Public Aid is even worse. Federally run programs are a disaster. They don't work in a cost effective or fiscally prudent manner.

CHAPTER 3

Medicare Funding: At Long Last, Free Healthcare! Not So Fast! It's Not All Free and It's Not All Covered! (and It's Broken Anyway)

Your Medicare benefits don't necessarily coincide with your age at retirement. You're eligible for Medicare benefits at age 65; however, you may not; in fact probably won't retire until after that age. I'm currently at a point in my life where I must make a decision about how I want my healthcare coverage to be handled. What could be better? Here I am; a perfect poster child for this part of my book. I can already see, from a cursory glance at the Medicare handbook there are a lot of hitches, glitches and penalties built into the system. You can find the handbook on the internet by typing "Medicare Beneficiary Hand Book" in your internet browser bar.

Just when you thought you were going to slack off from any heavy mental lifting because you're finally retired, you discover that you're going to have to navigate your way through an alphabet soup of Medicare options in order to make informed choices. Medicare policy coverage is split up into several parts and each of those separate parts is designated with a letter of the alphabet. Even if you combine all of the separate parts of Medicare, you still won't have full medical coverage.

First rule: Look out for deadlines. If you don't enroll when Medicare wants you to, they will punish you for your slothfulness. You may have to pay penalties for enrolling late and you may have to go uninsured until their enrollment period opens again. Why? Are Federal employees like teachers or construction workers who only work seasonally?

Second rule: Never ask any Federal employee "Why". You'll make them very uncomfortable because they're clueless in the "why" Department. You can ask them "when, where and how" and you'll most likely get the information you need, but back off that "why" stuff because the only answer you'll ever get is "because it's the rule" or "it's the law". If you try moving up the Medicare supervisory food chain to get an answer, it's going to be the same. All training of Federal employees takes place under the guidance of The Lemming Law Principle. If you are a "why" person, you can't work meaningfully with the Federal government.

It's very important that you understand exactly how Medicare services are either paid for or not, as the case may be. Once you understand the system, you'll understand why many healthcare providers opt not to enroll in the Medicare System as providers or severely limit the number of Medicare patients they'll render care to in their practices. Many providers are simply at a point where it is no longer financially feasible to provide your medical care. They're not greedy and unsympathetic. They simply cannot cover their costs with Medicare reimbursement payments and would go out of business if they continued to accept low Medicare rates of reimbursement.

Every year, the Feds (CMS or The Center for Medicare and Medicaid Services) review the medical reimbursement system, make changes and determines how much they'll pay for each and every service and piece of equipment that could possibly be utilized in the healthcare provider setting. Each item or service has a code attached to it which was created by the American Medical Association (more about the AMA in the last chapter of this book) and each of those codes comes with a price tag attached to it. Not only is their a price tag, there are rules, regulations, caveats and God knows what else attached to that code which determines whether or not it will be paid. Then there is the amount of money the Feds are willing to pay for that specific equipment or service code. This is called a Physicians Fee Schedule and is updated and published each year. In this current year (2010), the fee schedule only covers about six months and is an issue of some lively debate in congress. As you may remember, during the hot and heavy debate over Obamacare, one of the cost cutting measures was to reduce the amount of money paid to all healthcare providers who accept Medicare as a pay source. The cost of Obamacare reflected this "cut" amount as a savings or reduction in the overall cost of the program in the new healthcare bill. Keep that thought in mind. It's important. No final decision was made and amazingly, **the cost of paying all healthcare provider fees was taken out of the equation** when the cost of passing Obamacare was calculated! So, Obamacare calculations did not include any of the actual cost of paying healthcare providers in the bill; however, they listed a dollar amount reduction for cutting those same fees in the total cost of healthcare. If the total payable cost was not in the equation, how could you include the reduction of that same cost in the budget? The Feds, in this case congress, simply cooked the books on the actual cost of healthcare. They didn't include the cost of paying healthcare providers for their services anywhere in the actual cost of providing Obamacare, just the amount they would save by cutting those fees. This is huge! The entire cost of providing your Medicare services was eliminated from the Federal budget calculations! Do you get it? The Feds deceived you. Fancy that!

The fee schedule, as it's called, is based upon an incredibly convoluted formula which includes the cost of living index. The president passed a temporary measure to continue payments for a short period of time (about six months) until the subject could be revisited and resolved. And guess what? The fees were reduced anyway. The Feds cited the drop in the cost of living as a reason to do so. Have any of you out there seen a decrease in the amount it costs you to survive on a daily basis? Many healthcare providers who accept Medicare payments are sitting on the fence right now; waiting to see what the Feds are going to do. Decrease those fees and more doctors are going to book! The amount of money the fee schedule assigns for payment does not cover the cost of equipment and services on a good day. Those fees are already lower than the costs to produce the market product! Healthcare providers who accept Medicare as a pay source are already accepting a financial loss when they agree to render care to Medicare recipients. They make up the differential by rendering care to privately insured patients where reimbursements are at or above the market cost of the product. That solution to the problem can only be stretched just so far.

I'm taking a break in this part of your Medicare education with a true story. – A little light reading may help you refocus when we resume your education about the Medicare system.

A very critically ill patient, newly enrolled in Medicare Parts A, B & D with an additional backup medigap insurance policy lands in a local hospital emergency room courtesy of the prompt lifesaving action of the local fire department. Upon arrival it was determined that she was having a heart attack and severe damage to her heart muscle was taking place. The local hospital was equipped to handle the patient's first line emergency medical care but did not have cardiac specialty care to provide the open heart surgery she would need to unclog or replace her coronary arteries. The ER started six IV drugs, multiple monitors, intubated her (placed an airway tube through her mouth and into her lungs), initiated mechanical ventilation to breath for her, inserted a foley catheter to collect urine, placed an NG tube through her nose to drain stomach contents, and then addressed her cardiac insufficiency by starting an intra-aortic balloon pump to reduce the work her heart was doing as it pumped. A really long, very skinny balloon (literally) was inserted though a large blood vessel in her groin and advanced all the way up near her aortic arch which is the first large blood vessel exiting her heart. Then they attached that balloon to a large pumping mechanism which inflated and deflated the balloon in a rhythmic manner timed to match her heartbeat. As you can imagine, it was difficult to find the patient in the jumble of all those tubes, lines and pieces of equipment. Ok; so far so good! She was stabilized; not cured by any means but out of immediate danger as long as all of the newly initiated care could be continued. Now, what to do next? She needed to be transferred to a hospital ten miles away that was able to do the surgery she needed. Call the fire department? Not a chance. They did their part. They have no idea how to handle most of the equipment the hospital started. Their ambulances are not set up to handle the equipment the ER placed in service to stabilize the patient. The solution was to call a private ambulance company who has the equipment, staff and technical expertise to handle this patient's medical needs safely. There are very few ambulance companies that have the resources to do this. My company is one of a very few that does. It took a five person crew; two paramedics, two nurses, and a respiratory therapist to get the job done. All hospital equipment had to be changed over to transport equipment so it could be continued on board the ambulance. This is a very time consuming process; however, once it was done, the transport of the patient commenced. Upon arrival at the receiving hospital, all that equipment was once again changed over to the receiving hospital's equipment. The transport team was tied up about four hours in all. Good news! The patient had her surgery and is doing well. We, her ambulance company then billed Medicare Part B for her medical services. Her bill calculated out to about $4500.00. Medicare then paid us just over $550.00 and assigned the patient about $180.00, leaving a very large unpaid balance on the books. The patient called us and wanted to know why her bill was only $180.00 and who was responsible for the unpaid portion of her bill. She assumed someone had made a mistake. When we told her that no one was responsible and that Medicare required that we write the balance off, she was floored. Her comment is the point of the story. She asked, "How in the world does the Federal government expect you to keep working if that's all you can be paid? You guys saved my life and you can't even get a decent amount of money? It's crazy! Something is very wrong with this system."

Understanding private insurance coverage looks like child's play; kindergarten, if you will, compared to navigating your way through the Medicare system of healthcare coverage. Most people who have Medicare coverage with all of its component parts are still uncertain exactly what additional coverage they may need to avoid financial devastation by a serious illness or accident. They have most likely purchased a Medigap policy to cover those expenses Medicare doesn't and are hoping for the best when they actually have occasion to use their healthcare benefits.

Medicare Part A, for the most part is free for those who have paid into the system over the course of their lives. For those who have not paid any funds in, Part A may still be purchased in some cases. However,

Medicare Parts B and D as well as Medigap coverage all must be paid for out of the retiree's pocket. What I've found out about this subject in my personal research as a potential Medicare consumer is that I may be far better off keeping a private self pay policy in effect rather than opting for any Federally funded programs. Since I have a high deductible and an extended copay percentage, the cost I'm paying for my private policy is not very much different than paying for Medicare Parts B and D; then paying for a Medigap Policy as well. This may not be a good financial strategy for everyone; however, you may want to keep this in mind when you're shopping for Medicare coverage at age 65. Another benefit that keeping my private policy brings to the table is simply that doctors who will not accept Medicare as a pay source are still available to me. In future, that may be a powerful bargaining chip I can bring to the table if and when I am faced with the need for any expensive medical procedures. The rationing of healthcare, which I expect to see escalate when Obamacare hits full swing makes the private market look far more attractive to me as a consumer.

Now we can proceed with the information you need in order to understand the Medicare system; insofar as is possible, and make a decision about how you want your Medicare coverage to be structured. All government supported healthcare coverage choices are full of deadlines, pitfalls and penalties; caveats, restrictions and twisted rules too numerous to list here. You may need the assistance of family members or other seniors who have already painfully navigated the system. Some of the most glaring pitfalls and penalties are included here; however, make certain you have the government handbook as a starting point in your search. If you have access to the internet, you can type "Medicare & You 2010" in your internet browser bar to access the online version. If you don't have access to the internet, call 1-800-MEDICARE (1-800-633-4227). TTY users should call 1-877-486-2048. The Medicare service representative should help you out or mail you a copy of the handbook.

Medicare Part A:

This is the freebie! If you (or your spouse) paid into Medicare you'll be able to get something back out. However, it's not likely to be what you thought you were going to get. This coverage is for your hospitalization or healthcare facility services only. It's a no frills policy and only what's absolutely necessary will be paid for. If the hospital charges for the TV in your room; slippers or a razor, you'll have to pay for those things on your own. There are also medical procedures that Medicare won't cover. Chief among those procedures are experimental ones. Even if the procedure saves your life, you're going to pay for it yourself if the Feds, (CMS again) haven't put it on the list of OK stuff to pay for. If CMS says no and you don't have the money, you can't have it unless the hospital and doctors are willing to write off the expenses. This isn't negotiable, period. If CMS says "no" then no matter who argues your case, the service won't be paid for. You're already in a rationing phase of healthcare as soon as you switch from private insurance to Medicare; a very serious rationing phase. You're now receiving socialized medicine.

Medicare Part A is for inpatient care; emphasis on the "in" part of patient care. It won't cover your ambulance trip or any other expense that you've incurred during your illness if the event occurred before you were admitted to the hospital or care facility as an inpatient. It also won't cover any expenses after you've been discharged from the care facility. If your doctor sent you over to the hospital outpatient radiology department for a chest X-ray and then you find out you have to hop on over to the ER because you're really pretty sick, your X-ray still will won't be covered because it's not a Part A expense. You had the X-ray before you were formally admitted to the hospital. Your emergency room care is also not considered part of your inpatient care either. I cannot stress strongly enough that Part A is for your inpatient stay expenses only and it doesn't cover everything. It also has a time limit. Medicare Part A will only pay for a certain number of days per medical event. After you've paid your deductible, the first 60 days you receive care in a medical facility are covered benefit days. The next 30 days, that is days 61 through 90 will cost you about $275.00 per day. After 90 days, the cost will increase to $550.00 per day until you have reached your 151st day. After your 150th day, you're financially on your own and responsible for all costs of your stay. If you don't get well enough to leave the facility in the correct time frame, you'll have to pay out of your own pocket for those days you remain admitted in the care facility beyond the Medicare limit. The time period you stay in a facility after your insurance coverage has either been reduced in payment amount or lapsed entirely, is called your **Medigap** period.

Once you've left the care facility, you still won't usually be covered for another 72 hours unless you do something like break a leg on the way home from your hospital stay. After being discharge, if you're readmitted to any hospital or care facility in less than 72 hours for the **same** illness, it's going to be a no-pay situation unless you have unused Medicare days left. However, that broken leg is a whole new and unrelated medical problem so it will most likely get you covered again. "Unrelated medical problem" is the qualifier in this event. Your broken leg is unrelated to the illness you were previously being treated for. It's a brand new medical event. This 72 hour rule set the Medicare Part A system up for some of the biggest and most expensive fraud imaginable (See the fraud and abuse section), and it was perpetrated by and large in the physician population; sometimes with the patient's knowledge and cooperation and sometimes without. Even with Medicare Part A insurance coverage, you'll still need a private insurance policy, paid for out of your own pocket for all the care you still need that Medicare Part A doesn't cover. Hold that thought in your head. Part A; not enough; get more insurance.

Medicare Part B: This isn't a freebie. If you want insurance coverage for medical care that takes place outside the hospital setting, you must purchase this insurance coverage separately just like any other insurance policy. The cost to do so is graduated and based upon your adjusted gross income. This policy only covers your outpatient services. Remember that X-ray you had in the outpatient department at the hospital before you were admitted and the care you received in the emergency room? This is the pay source. If you're taken to or from the hospital in an ambulance, visit your doctor's office or have outpatient therapy of some kind, Medicare Part B will be the pay source, provided the care you need is listed on the Medicare "can do" list. If you've chosen not to purchase this coverage, and don't have another policy in place to cover these services, you'll have to pay for your medical care out of your own pocket. Even if you do have this coverage, Medicare will only pay 80% of your bill. This is a **permanent** copay assignment. It never goes away and you'll always need to pay for the 20% of your care

Medicare does not cover. There are also excluded medical services that are not on that "can do" list and a modest deductible at the beginning of each calendar year. For FY 2010, the deductible was set at $155.00. Your deductible may, and probably will change each year. So, even with Medicare Part B coverage, you still have numerous uncovered expenses; chief among them is the 20% of all costs that Medicare Part B does not pay for. Hold that thought in your head. Part B; not enough; get more insurance.

Medicare Part D: This is your prescription drug policy and it's not a freebie either. This is another policy that you must pay for and the requirements for purchase are a little strange. If you don't elect to take prescription drug coverage at the same time that you enroll in Medicare Part A, you're going to pay a penalty when you finally do want the coverage. Don't ask why. It's the law. I take an occasional dose of over the counter Ibuprofen for occasional aches and pains attributable to my age. Nothing else; so I flat out don't need drug coverage. I haven't needed any prescription drugs in so many years; I can't even remember when I might last have taken them. Doesn't matter! If you think some day you might need a prescription drug, you have to start paying now. This policy has a stiffer deductible, small copays and a good size gap in coverage. The gap in coverage is, indeed very strange. First you must pay all deductible expenses before the policy begins paying for your drugs. Then Medicare Part D will begin paying your expenses. When you've satisfied your deductible and then reached benefit payments of about $2800.00 a strange thing happens. Your insurance disappears and you have to start paying for everything yourself until you've spent about $4550.00 of your own money in addition to your original deductible. Then, you go back to being insured until January 1 of the next year. You start all over again with the same process at the beginning of each year. Speaking of drugs, I'd like to know what kind of drugs the people who set this plan up were taking when they figured this one out.

Medicare Parts A, B and D coverage are provided by several different companies and you may have a different one from your sister who lives in another state. The insurers are regional and you'll need to do some research in your area to find out who they are and how to enroll. Your Medicare beneficiary line should be able to give you that information at the time you sign up for Medicare Part A. You'll most likely be pushed to purchase Part D coverage at the time you first enroll in any form of Medicare. If you are resistant or reluctant to commit at that time, you will be given a litany of dire consequences that will befall you if you don't knuckle under and purchase that policy. Medicare Part D, like parts A and B also leaves a lot of expenses unpaid. Hold that thought in your head. Part D; not enough; get more insurance.

Get the idea? Even when you receive Medicare benefits to the fullest extent available from the Federal government; polices that are "free" as well as those you pay for, you'll still need to purchase more insurance. You'll need a Medigap policy. At a minimum, your Medigap policy needs to cover all of those expenses that are not covered by Parts A, B and D. Be very careful which Medigap policy you purchase. Make certain it's actually going to cover gaps in all three Medicare policies; Parts A, B and D.

Medicare Part C: Yes, I'm aware that my alphabet is out of order. I needed to save this coverage explanation until last in order to allow for continuity in the presentation of information about government run Medicare programs. That is, insofar as continuity is possible in any government program.

Medicare Part C is **privatized** coverage. There are some parts of it that aren't really spectacular; that could be improved, but by in large, it's a simple, cost effective and relatively inexpensive way to manage healthcare for our seniors. Private insurance companies receive funding from the Federal government to manage this type of Medicare coverage, and then provide comprehensive care to our seniors at a very reasonable premium rate. It's actually a lot more complicated than that; however, for our purposes, the behind the scenes details are not really relevant to this discussion. The premium rate is in line with what seniors already pay to the Feds for Medicare Parts B and D as well as Medigap coverage. In some cases, the premiums may be somewhat higher with improved or additional benefits. This type of coverage is very comprehensive and enrollment is simpler and far easier to understand. Unlike Medicare A, B and D. it's one stop shopping. The private insurance system has worked this out in an efficient and cost effective manner and **is able**

to make a profit while adhering to all Medicare rules, unlike the Feds who made up all of the rules in the first place and still lose money.

This type of coverage is called Medicare Advantage or Medicare Replacement and is the type of insurance coverage that Obamacare is set to eliminate. I'm sure the Feds took one look at the bottom line on the financial statements of the insurance companies providing this coverage and said "wait a minute, we need to put this back into the hands of the Federal Government so we can get our hands on that profit!". If the Feds take back control and eliminate these policies, the bureaucratic machine will simply eat up those profits and generate more expenses leading to more losses anyway. It's what the Feds do best! The last I heard, Obamacare will eliminate these policies throughout the United States with the exception of Florida. Why Florida? Obamacare needed to have Florida's congressional senate vote in order to pass. The elimination of these insurance policies may have changed several times by now. No one is quite certain where the ever changing Obamacare deals stand at any moment in time. Dirty deeds and deals; that's what Obamacare is composed of!

Not all Medicare replacement policies are equal. If you're going to enroll in one, make certain of one thing. Ask if reimbursement is only paid when you use the insurer's network providers or if there is a penalty for going out of network. Your insurance company should pay any provider who is contracted with the Feds to provide Medicare services. Most reputable insurance companies who provide this type of insurance coverage will pay any provider who has contracted with the Federal Government to provide healthcare to Medicare recipients and will pay at Medicare established rates. As much as I dislike and distrust Humana, whom I will totally trash later in this book, they handle their Medicare replacement program in this manner and their insured patients don't seem to have any major difficulties with the insurance program particulars. If any Medicare replacement insurance provider tells you that you must only use their network, or they will not pay a non-network provider, run like the proverbial bat out of hell! Their premiums will be cheaper, but they will destroy you with unpaid bills. Remember, if it looks too good to be true folks; it is. That lower cost is obtained by these companies in an interesting manner. They contract with hospitals and healthcare providers at **below market** reimbursement rates; below what Medicare usually pays so their provider base is limited. Medicare reimbursement to healthcare providers is already well below the market value of the service so not many high quality providers are willing to go lower. Then, when care is rendered to you by a caregiver who is not in their network, you're screwed. Private insurance companies negotiate lower rates with providers on a regular basis; however, most Medicare replacement policy insurers are smart enough not to try this with Medicare Federally funded plans. The Feds were not bright enough to make this practice illegal; therefore they have no control over this situation. Many Medicare recipients have found out the hard way that they don't have full medical coverage.

Medicare Part C is clearly Medicare insurance cleaned up and simplified for our seniors. It was simplified and reorganized into a workable, reasonably priced system by the **private business** sector.

If you're a Medicare recipient with both Part A and B coverage what should you expect to pay for on your own? First of all, remember that there are many services that Medicare will not fund. Chief among them are experimental procedures and anything that Medicare deems "not medically necessary" as well as outpatient prescription drugs if you don't have Part D coverage in addition to Parts A and B coverage. If you're uncertain about the coverage status of certain types of healthcare expenses or specific procedures and equipment, call your Medicare insurance company beneficiary line and ask them if the service you need is a covered benefit. The phone number to call is found on your Medicare insurance card.

It's important for you to understand that if you're taken to the closest hospital in an emergent situation, you'll need to stay in that hospital for the duration of your care as long as they have the means to provide for you. For instance, if you're in a hospital where your primary care physician is **not** on staff, Medicare will **not** pay the cost of your transport to a hospital where your physician practices. It doesn't matter if your doctor requests the transfer; it's still not going to be paid for. If you don't like the care you are receiving and want to move to another hospital, once again, you'll have to pay for a transfer on your own. If Medicare does not cover these expenses, neither will a Medicare backup policy or a Public Aid supplement. Once Medicare denies payment of any care or service, that care will be denied by your other insurers as well. You're financially on your own in such situations. Your ambulance transport company should tell you in advance that you'll have to pay out of your own pocket and they often require cash up front before the transport can take place. Paying for an ambulance transport out of your own pocket is very expensive.

You should also expect to pay an annual deductible out of your own pocket and 20% of any outpatient expenses if you don't have a Medicare backup policy. If you do have a backup policy, make certain it covers Medigap days or you'll also have to pay for that. Again, I cannot stress this enough; call your insurance company and ask them if they cover some of these expenses. Shop around for the best coverage your budget will allow. Despite the fact that you have Medicare coverage, you may still have devastatingly large bills which fall into a Medicare black hole labeled "not medically necessary" or "not a covered benefit".

The last thing we need to cover in this section is the Medicare appeal process which you may need to utilize if Medicare denies coverage of a medical procedure and you don't agree with their decision. If your care was not paid for based on Medicare **rules**, or statutory limitations which have been clearly explained, you most likely don't have a case. These are rules of law and as such, are not flexible for any reason no matter how compelling your situation. If non-payment is based upon an **opinion** about whether or not your care was medically necessary, you stand a much better chance of success if you're willing to go the distance through the appeal process. That distance can be lengthy, time consuming, frustrating and cumbersome.

The first thing you'll need to do is call your Medicare insurance carrier and ask them to explain why payment was denied and how to get started on an appeal. You should also call the healthcare provider who submitted the bill for services on your behalf and let them know that you're already "on the case". They may be able to provide you with information that will strengthen your chances of success. If I'm your healthcare provider, I'll most likely file a simultaneous appeal on your behalf. Do not give up easily.

The Medicare appeal process is absolutely ridiculous, far more difficult and cumbersome than an appeal in the private insurance sector and much less likely to succeed. The government appeal process structure is extremely expensive to maintain (on the taxpayers dime no less) since it requires large numbers of employees who have been placed on taxpayer funded payrolls to process appeals. I've had hundreds of appeal cases which may, and often do last as long as two years, tie up four separate review appeal levels and eventually are placed before an Administrative Law Judge before someone (the Judge and his associate attorneys) makes an intelligent decision. I don't give up easily, nor should you. I've only lost four or five cases in my career. Is it worth the time and trouble? No, absolutely not! I usually end up with $80.00 to $200.00 per case; it's the principle of the whole process that matters. Why does the case ultimately need to be decided by a Judge? Simply because the "medical professionals" who were hired by your Medicare insurance group (and CMS) to review your case are not the sharpest knives in the drawer. Most of these "medical professionals" don't have sufficient background knowledge to review your case. If they did, your case wouldn't have to go to a Judge. When an Administrative Law Judge finally finds that the charges should be paid based on medical necessity and/or rule of law, it certainly indicates the previous review groups didn't know enough about the subject to render an accurate decision; either from a medical standpoint or a legal one. So, don't give up. Each time you receive a negative response, ask what the next level of appeal is and soldier on.

In the previous chapter, private healthcare insurance coverage was defined and explained. By now, the reader should have come to the conclusion that private insurance coverage is very simple compared to Medicare or Federal coverage. That's what happens when you let the Federal government run much of anything. If there's a way to complicate or screw it up, the Feds will do it. So, of course, I have a plan of my own. The following are my recommendations.

First of all, privatize all Federally funded healthcare programs. Don't just privatize them, form an independent, non-government supported, limited profit corporation to handle all income from premiums as well as the taxes being paid into Medicare by working Americans to support this program. This same group should control all benefit payments.

Place very strict restrictions into the system and set up an oversight committee to monitor all activity. Place tight criteria on who can become a member of the oversight committee and how long they can serve in that position. Private insurance companies such as Humana are making profits in the Medicare replacement policy business using taxpayer funds. They are managing their resources very well, following Medicare guidelines and still making a profit. They have also implemented safety nets to catch much of the fraud and abuse that the federal government can't seem to control. Use them as a model and then either eliminate them or have the really good ones take the entire system over. They have it figured out. Privatize the system and it will be more cost effective with improved coverage as well as fiscally prudent management. Maybe Medicare funds will last a little longer.

My second recommendation is to combine all levels of Medicare coverage and charge for it at a combined rate, rather than charging for bits and pieces of additional or optional coverage along the way. Base the monthly premiums on an equitable amount that would be paid out in total by the insured and would be similar to the amount usually paid to a Medigap insurer, a Part B insurer and for Part D prescription drug coverage. In short, make it a full policy. And lastly, charge for that combined insurance coverage on a graduated scale based on a household's **gross** income. If the gross household income is below a designated level, forget Medicare altogether and enroll the recipient in Public Aid. And don't establish the payment threshold at some ridiculously high amount of money. Everyone who possibly can, should contribute, at least a little something to the system. Allow open enrollment three month before **retirement** age, not age 65 and knock off the stupid penalties for late enrollment. Keep early enrollment exceptions in place for chronically or catastrophically ill recipients who qualify for early benefits. Establish a reasonable deductible and copay schedule also based on household **gross** income. End Stage Renal Disease and Hospice Care payments which currently fall into special Medicare categories should be handled in the same manner as all other medical care payments. If the patient's gross income falls below a given level, why not automatically enroll them in Public Aid for coverage? Forget about those Medigap days. You know, those gaps in coverage when all of a sudden, your Medicare coverage disappears for a time and then suddenly shows up on the horizon again later. Now the only other insurance that might be needed by our seniors would be vision and dental. Let the private insurance companies have at it for that limited coverage only. How much more simplified can you get and still enable every one of our seniors to participate in some kind of reasonable, cost effective coverage based on their ability to pay?

Most Patients in long term extended care facilities have no funds available for insurance premiums and receive Medicare Part A benefits only with Public Aid Backup. Or, they are completely dependent upon Public Aid funding because they never paid into the Medicare system. They're already in a totally free healthcare zone. They pay nothing into the system. If someone has an income that falls below a preset threshold, they should be, and usually are covered by Public Aid funding anyway. I prefer a heavy dose of coverage by Public Aid. If we stopped giving Public Aid away at the blink of an eye for stupid entitlement programs that half the recipients don't deserve anyway, there would be enough to enable funding for what's really necessary, like taking care of our seniors who once were taking care of us.

In the day to day management of my company, I see more fraud and abuse in Public Aid funding than in any other area of healthcare and entitlement funding, and it's being perpetrated by the American and not so very American public alike. This is one of the goodies bringing illegal immigrants into this country in droves. Medicare funding is falling further and further behind in its ability to self fund. Public Aid entitlement programs are breaking the financial backs of our States. If we don't start getting some meaningful cash on the books and develop a system of prudent, fiscally responsible distribution, these benefits are not going to be around long. The Federal government has already repeatedly demonstrated its inability to operate in a fiscally prudent manner; therefore we should not allow them to continue down the same path toward certain bankruptcy of the Medicare system. The Obamacare system of healthcare is set to reduce benefits to seniors and increase entitlement funding through Public Aid to many people in this country who have never even paid into the system.

The last and certainly most important thing that must be done to secure the future of Medicare funding is to see to it that the Feds can't touch the money set aside for healthcare funding for any reason. The working American public pays into this fund to enable this program to currently exist and support the cost of their future healthcare needs. The Feds should never be allowed to shift those funds for any other uses not related to the provision of healthcare. In the private business sector, such activities might well be labeled embezzlement.

Chapter 4

Public Aid Funding: What Funding? It looks More Like 50% Waste, Fraud and Abuse To Me!

The polite term for Public Aid funded medical care is Medicaid. Most healthcare providers prefer to call it what it is. The term Medicaid is far too similar to the term Medicare and is often confused with the latter. Public Aid funding is financial aid provided to the recipient of that aid by the tax paying public through both State and Federal Taxes. That's right, if you pay both State and Federal taxes, you are paying twice to assist in this program. You get whacked coming and going.

State taxes fund about one half of the cost of this program. The Federal Government matches that cost and kicks in the other half needed to pay the expenses. The money the feds are kicking in is not without conditions; really big conditions. The States must meet Federal criteria to get that funding. There are a huge number of entitlement programs that the State must provide in order to qualify for Federal funding whether the State wants to provide those services or not. If the State won't provide what the Feds insist upon, their Federal funding can be cut off. Obamacare increases Public Aid mandates in an enormous way which places an additional burden on the States, most of whom are already broke. This, of course places a heavy burden on the taxpayers of the State. The States will ultimately have no choice other than to raise your taxes to fund these additional freebie programs. Some of these programs are very worthwhile, while some are no more than expensive con games.

The taxpayers of this country are literally being crushed under the weight of this massive, under funded, misused and corrupt system. Why do you think many States have consistently increased their taxes and are now faced with cutting costs in other areas of their budgets? Areas that may well be of more benefit to the State and its citizens. Do you really think that the Feds are not going to come after more from every taxpayer out there in order to meet their promise of reimbursement for entitlement programs to the States?

Most recipients of Public Aid believe it's "free". Since the State pays for the services, they feel that if they lie, steel and cheat to get it, it's OK. They view it as a victimless crime. Nothing could be further from the truth. The entire working, tax paying population of this country is being systematically victimized by these thieves. To those of you who are valid recipients of Public Aid with a clearly demonstrated need, I willing and gladly give it to you. To those of you who are not valid recipients, I despise you for the lowlife blood sucking thieves that you are. There! Is my position clear enough for you on this subject? Just wait until I tell you what I really think in the fraud and abuse section of this book.

Just how does Public Aid work? It doesn't! Work that is! It's an abysmal, wasteful failure and is driving the Federal government and our States into bankruptcy. Most people in this country are not opposed to giving the needy an occasional hand up when they're in dire straights through no fault of their own. The American people are, by and large a generous people and don't have any problem helping the truly needy. We have a long history of bailing out the entire world in times of disaster and great need; but there are the needy and then there are the greedy. It's the free candy that does it. You get your free candy and then get in line again and again for more. You are addicted to it. Guys; we're running out of free candy!

Philosophical ideology creates an enormous political divide over the issue of entitlement programs; Left vs. Right, Democrat vs. Republican.

Liberal vs. Conservative. The left side, or Democrats believe that all Republicans are mean, greedy, selfish and don't want to help anyone. The right side or Republicans believe that Democrats are unrealistic, fiscally irresponsible batty dreamers who operate on the Robin Hood principle and will drive this country into bankruptcy. Nothing is going to change that ideological perspective. You either buy into one side or the other; or perhaps you are sane enough to realize each side has its valid points. It's an argument older than the founding of this country and is not likely to change or go away. There's an old saying which states something to the effect that we should never argue about politics or religion because no one will ever definitively win. If you want to stay out of the firestorm, you would do well to adhere to that old adage. You're not going to agree, so move forward and find **common** ground. Obamacare is **NOT** common ground. It is left wing ideology at its worst.

The ideological argument is not worth having in most cases. Political considerations drive the argument more often than do humanitarian aspirations. Underneath the concept of healthcare, it's largely about politics. It's all about "how can I get the vote". A politician must mobilize his base first; Democrat or Republican. Then, he must energize those undecided voters whom he thinks he can persuade to vote for him. The politician must get those voters to the polls. How does he do it? One of the old tried and true methods is to promise anyone and everyone something for nothing. Free candy! Politicians consistently refer to energizing certain voting groups and campaign exhaustively for that purpose. These groups are divided into specific voting blocks such as Hispanics, African Americans, Gays or Independents. Then the politician speaks to that groups unique needs and tells them what they want to hear; promises them specific goodies; their favorite candy. In the early days of political stumping, this method worked extremely well. Now, in the age of the internet and computerized information, trying to get elected with this method may be political suicide. This was clearly illustrated when Mr. Obama thought he was speaking privately to a California audience and slammed the people of Pennsylvania for clinging to their guns, bibles and religion.

Entitlement programs are very high up on the list of legal bribes used to obtain votes. Promise them what they want to hear and if you can actually deliver, even marginally on that promise, you're golden! Politicians Beware! You're in a whole new political arena of awareness and you would do well to remember that governing is "of the people, by the people and for the people". We have a very young, naive and inexperienced President. He's really not what we thought we were getting and he's not perceived as behaving in a fiscally responsible manner. He's certainly not listening to the overwhelming majority of the people. Unfortunately, he's behaving less like a President and more like a boy in a toy store who blew his entire allowance on his first shopping trip. All politicians should pay attention to what the majority of the voting public in this country wants done. If they don't, the American voting public will crucify them at the polls. The majority of the voting public is very tired of paying for wasteful entitlement programs. If the Federal government wants the support of the American public, it had better get busy and support the wishes of that same American public in turn. Public Aid entitlement spending is a rapidly growing malignant cancer in the collective bodies of the American tax paying citizens. We need some serious fiscally responsible financial chemotherapy treatments to cure the problem.

When you provide healthcare for a living, Public Aid scams make you so angry that it sometimes becomes impossible not to harbor enormous resentment toward the recipients as well as the system. Fortunately, most healthcare providers can ignore or step back from pay source issues and remain focused on the medical issues at hand. We can remind ourselves that some of these people really need our help. If we're unable to do that, we simply cease to provide care to Public Aid recipients and those who truly have a demonstrated need may be irreparably damaged. We really need to get this straightened out in order to continue helping the truly valid needy!

How do you get Public Aid? It's easy. You'll need to visit your local Medicaid office. You can find this information online by typing "Medicaid Information for States" in the search bar of your internet browser. There, I just made it even easier, didn't I! If you don't have access to a computer, most libraries have them available for public use. When you've located a Public Aid office nearby, you'll have to fill out an application and then you'll be notified whether or not you qualify.

Whether we like it or not, Public Aid is handed out freely. Remember, there are Federal mandates that **insist** upon handing out large amounts of it. If you don't qualify for Public Aid initially, many employees at the Medicaid offices will tell you how to get around the rules. No one cares if you're a legal resident of this country or not. No one cares if you're literate or have any understanding of the English language or not. No one cares if you've only been in this country 24 hours. No one cares if you've never contributed productively to this country. You want Public Aid? You can get it. The American taxpayers will be glad to hand it over to you. They have nothing better to do with their hard earned money.

Ok, here's what you may be told when you go to apply. You and your husband make too much money. Get divorced, have mom list the children as dependents and claim she has no idea where her children's father is; despite the fact that he is gainfully employed, living in the same household and has healthcare insurance through his employer. If you do that, we can give you every item on the Public Aid menu. Every item on the menu is huge. Everyone who reads this book should visit their State Medicaid websites to see what your tax dollars are paying for. It's a real eye opener. In the fraud and abuse section of this book, you're going to get an ear, make that an eye full of examples of Public Aid abuse.

Why do so many healthcare providers refuse to accept patients with Public Aid funding? It's very simple to understand. First of all, many States can't pay their bills. The healthcare providers have to wait months and months to collect a truly paltry sum for the services they've provided. That paltry sum being paid to them is the second reason. The ambulance industry in the State of Illinois has not received any increases in Pubic Aid reimbursement in more than a decade. Healthcare facilities are no better off. Recently, after having waited for months, my company received a check for just over $34,000.00 from the State. That check covered Public Aid bills which amounted to more than $550,000.00 over a six month period. That's right, more than a half million dollars. Do the math. We received just over six cents for every dollar of billed expenses. Do you recall that nice lady with the heart attack that we told you about in the Medicare chapter? You know: the case where it took a five man team to transport her for cardiac surgery? If she'd had Public Aid as a pay source, we would have received $225.00 and waited at least five or six months just to get that. Healthcare providers know that providing medical services to Public Aid recipients is fiscal suicide.

There's only one way for healthcare providers to stay in business. They have to find the money elsewhere. Medicare won't work because it's controlled at a fixed rate by the Feds and also reimburses below cost at about thirty five to forty five cents on the dollar. So, you want to know how we keep it all together. Guess what? All of you out there who are paying State and Federal taxes, probably also have private healthcare insurance. Our bills to your insurance companies reflect the average sums that we absolutely must be reimbursed from somewhere to stay in business. Need I say more? Why do you think your insurance policy is so expensive? Your insurance company has to charge you high premiums to pay for the bills you incur from the healthcare providers. You're not only getting hit coming and going, but now we are whacking you down sideways! But don't get up yet. We're going to slap you down one more time. You still have to pay us for your deductibles, copays and non-covered services. That's right! The working class American taxpayer and the private insurance companies are really paying for it all; Medicare and Public Aid funding bring in a pittance.

Taxing the rich is supposed to get us out of this? There're aren't enough rich people to even begin to get us out of this. Obamacare will send the costs experienced by the private insurance companies even higher through the roof resulting in ever increasing premium rates and decreasing reimbursements. What a mess! So, should we socialize the entire medical system and accept a corrupted level of care with rationing and long lines of people waiting for services? No, there's a better solution! Stop handing it out to every Tom, Dick and Harry who has no intention of ever contributing productively to the economy of this country. If you stop handing out that free candy, there won't be anyone standing in line for it. They'll be out working for a living out of necessity! They'll stop bearing children they can't feed, house, cloth or educate. They'll stop coming into the country illegally to get that candy. I'm willing to help anyone who's truly in need but I'm tired of being suckered by someone else's greed.

Chapter 5

What's An EOB? I Have No Idea How My Insurance Company Did This! Help! I Don't Know What This Says! I Can't Pay This!

We hear those questions and comments every day. An EOB is an Explanation of Benefits, or in many cases, a lack thereof. Each time your insurance company pays your medical bills, they issue an explanation of benefits listing what bills they've paid on your behalf. It doesn't really explain anything because it doesn't address any of those "why" issues we discussed previously. It does, however tell you how much of your bill has been paid, or not as the case may be. I highly recommend that you're always seated whenever you open any mail from your insurance company. If you become lightheaded when you see how much money you owe. Stick your head down between your knees. Your in a mild state of shock which should pass quickly only to be replaced by sheer outrage. Remember one thing. Even though your bill for services will come from your provider, they have absolutely no control over the costs incurred to provide your care or the amount your insurance carrier did or did not pay. They're stuck in the middle between the insurers and the patients; the proverbial rock and hard place.

Explanations from each of the insurance categories, private, Medicare and Public Aid are handled a little differently. Additionally, you're EOB and the healthcare provider's EOB may not look the same at all.

Many insurance companies actually do go to some additional efforts when reporting payments to the patients to make the subject easier to understand. The EOB issued to the healthcare provider is abbreviated with numerous codes the patient would not readily understand. It's expected that the provider will be able to decode these statements and handle any unpaid balances in an appropriate manner. Each of the three major sources of payment in the healthcare industry; private insurance, Medicare and Public Aid have some differences in their EOBs. The insurer documents payments in a specific format dictated by the terms of your policy. Your Medicare EOB will look very different from the EOB that was provided by your Medicare backup or Medigap insurance company.

Private Insurance EOBs:

If your policy is an HMO, your insurance company will determine if the healthcare service you received is a covered benefit and if so, they will generally pay line item for line item in full as long as the charges are not wildly exorbitant. The EOB will list each line item charge and how much was paid for each of those items. Anything left unpaid should be explained. If not, call your insurance company and ask for an explanation. If they determine the care was not needed, there will be no payment at all. HMOs usually require that you use a healthcare provider in their network with the exception of an emergency situation. In an emergency, these policies pay very well regardless of whether you've used a network provider or not. Private insurance company HMO policies are mandated by law to pay in emergent situations regardless of who provides your healthcare; whether the provider is contracted with the HMO or not. If you use a non-network provider in a non-emergent setting, most HMOs will still pay for the healthcare you received as long as that care meets payment criteria and charges are reasonable. My company does not contract with any private insurance companies. Contracts can and often do lead to significant abuse (usually to the patient) of the system and often smack of kickbacks (more about this in the fraud and abuse section of this book). Certain insurance companies engage in horrendous abusive practices while others are quite equitable. In this regard, HMOs are usually much cleaner than PPOs. They're very straightforward with payment issues. If the service provided to you is a covered benefit, it gets paid; if not, no reimbursement will be forthcoming and they rarely quibble over payments in emergency situations.

If your policy is a PPO, your EOB will be far more complicated. A PPO insurer's EOB will list the total amount billed by the healthcare provider, the amount that the insurer will accept as payable (covered services), the amount they will not consider for payment (not covered services), the amount applied to the patients deductible, the amount of the patients copay and the final amount they are paying to your provider.

Let's say you're in your deductible insurance phase with $500.00 left unpaid for your responsibility, there is $600.00 in not covered charges and you have an 80/20 copay. If your bill for services was $3800.00, your benefits will be calculated somewhat similar to the following formula:

Covered Amount = Billed Amt of $3800.00 – $600.00 Not covered service

Payable amount = (Covered Amt X .80) - $500.00 Deductible

For those of you who don't speak math, here's the same thing in English.

The payment amount will be equal to the amount billed minus services that your insurance carrier does not consider payable ($600.00), leaving $3200.00 that will be used for payment calculation. The payable $3200.00 will then be reduced by 20% for your copay, which is equal to $640.00 and then reduced again by your $500.00 deductible.

Your full unpaid balance is the sum of $600.00 for not covered charges, $500.00 for your deductible and $640.00 for your copay which is equal to a total of $1740.00. Ouch! If your copay and deductible had both already been satisfied, you would still have the not covered charges of $600.00 to pay for. Not covered services are a big deal when it comes to how much you owe your healthcare provider and most patients don't even realize that these charges exist until they see their bills. Then they're furious with the healthcare provider. Hey! We didn't sell you the policy and we have no idea what yours is going to cover (or not) so don't yell at us. We're not too thrilled about those unpaid charges either. When you call your insurance company, they're going to tell you we didn't bill correctly; that we should have "bundled" or added all of our charges together in a lump sum. Don't let them fool you. We've billed both ways; with our charges bundled and separated. The insurance company pays the exact same amount no matter which method we use and they assign the exact same unpaid balance to you. Therefore, we bill our charges with each billed item or service listed separately so everyone clearly sees exactly what services were provided, billed for and not separately covered by your insurer. I believe our billing method would be labeled transparent.

As a consumer, you do have one weapon in your arsenal against your insurance company when you believe they haven't paid correctly. Once you've exhausted all appeal rights with your insurer, you can appeal your case with your State Insurance Board. Type the name of your State or whichever State you wish to contact and access their website. In order to do that, your internet browser bar should look something like this: "www.indiana.gov" with your State replacing the word "indiana". Be patient. Once you've found your State website, it sometimes takes a while to find the insurance board sub-site and figure out how to file an appeal. Before you actually file your appeal, talk your bill over with both your healthcare provider and your insurance company. They may be able to give you some pertinent information that will help your cause. You'll need to present a detailed, well documented, organized case in order to have any hope of success. Just filing a complaint because you don't like your bill, is not going to do you much good. You need to state clearly why you think your services were not paid correctly. If you're not comfortable with the internet process, ask your healthcare provider's billing department for the phone number of your State's insurance board. Tell them what you plan to do so they can assist you in any way possible. Your provider should be able to look up the State Insurance Board telephone number for you. Many insurance companies actually list this information on the bottom or back side of your explanation of benefits and that will certainly save you time. So check there first. You may not win your case; however, if it's well presented and rational, it will be investigated. It's certainly worth a shot.

There are some insurance companies, or specific types of policies which do not allow direct payment to the healthcare provider. Even though your healthcare provider performed the service for you, obtained a signature from you authorizing them to bill on your behalf, and then billed your insurance carrier, the insurer will still send the check to you. This leads to serious problems for the healthcare provider and the patient. This is not free money. If you are wise, you will not cash the check and spend it. The check should be endorsed over to the healthcare provider and forwarded to them along with the EOB that accompanied the payment. This happens regularly with policies held by Federal employees. In 95% of these cases, the patient takes the money and doesn't pay for their healthcare services.

What happens when you do that? You're very quickly sued. An attorney will haul you into court where you'll face a judge who isn't going to be even marginally sympathetic to you. Now you'll also have to pay all court and lawsuit costs. If your insurance company only sent a check to you for 70% of the bill, you'll still be sued for 100% of the billed charges and the entire cost of the court case. Understandably, our attorney will have no mercy in such a situation, nor will the judge. If you can't pay because you spent the money, the attorney will do something really ugly like garnishing your wages or worse, placing a lean against your home. If we lean your property, you can't sell it unless you satisfy the lean. My company has had more than one phone call from an irate patient who tried to sell his home only to have the deal fall through because he had a lean show up against the title on his home. Will a Judge find your story so compelling that he decides in favor of you? No; even if you tell the Judge that your husband died, you don't have a job, your home is in foreclosure and your children are starving. The Judge must determine your case based on rule of law. And anyway, this is nothing more than common theft. It's no different than robbing your local White Hen and then telling a jury your sad tale with the expectation that you're going to get off scott free. You're not a sympathetic figure to anyone regardless of your sad tale of woe. You're a thief.

Many people think that if they go into court over unpaid healthcare bills, the Judge will find in their favor because their story is so overwhelmingly tragic, sad and so much worse than anyone else's case. As sad and tragic as your case may well be, remember, everyone else has a similar story. Healthcare providers are faced with situations such as yours all day and every day. It's an industry built on tragedy. If a tragic story ruled out the ability of healthcare providers to collect their fees, there would soon be no one to provide care in the future because much of the work we do would go unpaid. We'd rapidly go out of business.

Your healthcare providers still have to pay their bills. Their employees can't work for free. They have families of their own to feed, clothe, educate and house. Your healthcare providers have financial responsibilities just like everyone else. They incur huge expenses in order to render care to you. Back to the basic premise I started with. It's a business, not a funded charity and if the services are not paid for, the healthcare provider is going to be out of business. The Judge must make his decision based on rule of law, not sympathy. Every month, my company is compelled to turn over 40 to 60 cases to our attorney. In the ten years I've been in business, I've lost in court only twice. I don't like to go to court but will do so whenever necessary.

So, what should you do when you can't pay your bills? First of all, don't ignore them. They're not going to go away. In fact, they'll come back to haunt you ten fold. If a friend or acquaintance tells you just to ignore them because it's no big deal, they're giving you very bad advice. We turn **every** unpaid bill over to our attorney and pursue all slackers to the fullest extent allowed by law. Contact your healthcare provider and try to work out some kind of payment arrangement. Then call your insurance carrier. Explore any means possible to get additional funds from them to cover the unpaid portion of your bill. Be sure to keep your healthcare provider in the loop and report on any progress. If I'm your healthcare provider, I'll make every effort to work with you. After all, we both have the same objective. We both want the insurance company to pay. If we can't make that happen, we'll review the specifics of your case and see if there's anything that can be done with the balance you owe. Don't expect us to just make your bill go away. That happens only under very rare circumstances and your case will most likely not be one of them. We may, however be able to waive some; mind you not all charges your insurance company won't consider for payment and we will most likely give you interest free time payments. If the balance you owe is for deductibles or copays you will have to pay the full amount for those items. The vast majority of healthcare providers won't give you a write off at all; however, if you work with them you'll be able to pay off your balance over time. It may not be interest free, but the interest should be reasonably low. Do not blow this deal. This kind of offer is only made once and you'll need to demonstrate good faith in order to keep that discount on the table. Blow the deal, you lose the discount and we'll see you in court for the full amount of the bill plus court costs.

Medicare EOBs:

Medicare EOBs are very cut and dried. Master one and you're done trying to figure anything else out. Your EOB should list the amount of the healthcare provider's bill, the total fee that Medicare will allow the provider to collect, the amount that the provider must write off, the amount that Medicare will actually pay and the amount left for the patient or their backup insurer to pay. Let's look at another case.

A 65 year old male is critically injured in an automobile accident. After the fire department cuts him out of his vehicle with JAWS, stabilizes him on a backboard, collars his neck and starts an IV for fluid delivery, they rush the victim to the nearest hospital emergency room. The ER staff stabilizes his crushed chest, places an airway tube through his mouth into his lungs and initiates a mechanical ventilator to breath for him. They start IV cardiac drugs to help correct the malfunction of his heart caused by his chest injury, hang several units of blood and fluids to replace the volume he's loosing due to internal injuries, reduce his bilateral femur fractures, insert a computerized catheter fluid line just below the midline of his right collar bone and advance it into his heart attaching the external end to special monitoring devices as well as pressurized bags of fluids. They insert a catheter to collect his urine, insert another catheter through his nose into his stomach which is returning a lot of bright red blood from abdominal injuries and, after all that, find upon X-ray and CT scan that the victim has a closed head injury. Uh Oh! Now we have a problem! The hospital doesn't provide neurosurgical services which the patient desperately needs. If you haven't figured it out yet, this patient is a critical mess facing imminent death. The likelihood of his survival is slim next to none. The head injury is actually his worst problem. Now what? Well, while someone is calling another hospital with neurosurgical services to see if they have a bed available for our patient, the ER doctor is going to start more drugs to keep the pressure in his head low which is rising due to swelling and bleeding of his brain tissue. Then the doctor will make sure that the patient is completely sedated so there is no further injury as a result of movement and pain. When that's complete, the hospital will begin the search for a medical team that has the sophisticated and I might add expensive resources available to transport the patient to the second hospital. The additional drug being given is diprivan or propofol; the anesthetic drug which became quite famous when Michael Jackson died from an overdose. Contrary to popular belief, our patient is quite safe with this drug since he's in the hands of professionals who are very well trained in its use. The patient is in luck. Not only is there a bed available in a hospital with neurosurgical services, there's also a full four person medical support team with the resources to transport him. The patient can't go by air because there is a vicious snowstorm going on (hence the accident) so the transport team must take the slower route through the storm. The patient (and his family) must trust that what remains of our patient's life is in good hands; that the driver of the ambulance for the critical care team knows what he's doing and is really very good at it. The distance is ten miles. Upon arrival in the emergency room of the sending hospital, the critical care team finds a bloody jumble of tubes, IV lines, monitors and life support equipment that's been placed in service in order to medically stabilize the patient. While the transport team is receiving an updated condition report from the ER staff, the patient destabilizes and drops his blood pressure to a dangerous low which is incompatible with life if left untreated. No one's going anywhere yet! The transport team remains on site and works with the ER staff to get the blood pressure back to an acceptable level for transfer. More drugs. Forty five minutes later, the patient is good to go with a stabilized blood pressure. That was a close call. We nearly lost him. The transport team can start the time consuming process of changing over all support systems, drug lines and monitors to their own equipment which will do the same thing on board an ambulance that's being done in the ER. When this is done, the transport team can barely find the patient amidst all of the lines, monitors and equipment, but he is on the ambulance cot and no longer tied to the ER bay by electrical and medical lines. The transport team loads the patient into the ambulance and starts the slow crawl through two feet of snow to the second hospital. Forget lights and sirens; no one's going anywhere in a hurry with such brutal driving conditions. During the transport, the patient destabilizes again, only this time his blood pressure soars to a dangerous high. The nurse on board the ambulance has the drugs, knowledge and equipment to handle this problem immediately and the patients blood pressure is rapidly, once again returned to a safe range. After a hair raising forty five minute trip, the transport team safely delivers the patient into the hands of the waiting neurosurgeon at the second hospital. All support systems, drugs and monitors are once again, transferred to hospital equipment and all the transport team has left to do is clean up their equipment (you can imagine what a bloody mess it must be) and complete their charting. They're finally free to return to their base; which is another thirty minute hair raising trip through the blizzard where they will remain until their next call from the dispatcher.

How did things go with this patient? Our critical care team kept in touch with hospital staff to see how things progressed during the course of his medical care. Since our crews are in and out of the second hospital on a regular basis to drop off other patients, they were regularly able to briefly pop in to see the patient and encourage him as well as his family members. Thankfully, against all odds, the patient made a nearly full recovery. It was a very difficult and bumpy medical road he had to travel, but he went the distance just the same. This case was documented to help the reader try and understand why we do this for a living. It's not a job. It's a vocation; a calling if you will. There are some things that transcend money. There's an intellectual, physical and emotional investment all rolled into the care of patients. This patient had virtually no chance of survival. We had to try. From those first line fire department rescuers through the entire medical course for this patient, healthcare providers were emotionally vested. They had to try. If it were about money, more than half of our patients would go wanting for care. The healthcare providers in this case all definitely lost money. Many people believe that patients should be evaluated for the likelihood of success and written of if the situation is too grim. This patient would have died in the emergency room of the first hospital if his care was based on whether or not he was likely to make a good recovery. We do not render healthcare based on the probability of a successful outcome as is done in most socialized countries.

This type of medical care is extremely expensive to provide and often doesn't end with such positive results. In fact, very few patients would have survived an episode such as this and returned to a productive life. No one in healthcare ever wants to see a case like this disallowed because a positive outcome is unlikely. No one ever wants to see healthcare decisions predicated on the probability of success. That's rationing of the worst kind and is unconscionable. There are those who believe that we should do just that. Ration healthcare based on a patient's likely potential for future productivity. They believe that funding this type of care has no realistic cost benefit.

Let's take a look at the money. No, I haven't lost my train of thought. I'm still on the same thread here. Our trauma patient was 65 years old, newly retired and had Medicare Part A, B and D coverage as well as a Blue Cross Blue Shield supplementary policy. He had adequate coverage *for a Medicare recipient.* His ambulance transports were Part B (or outpatient) services. Let's take a close look at those two ambulance transports he needed. The fire department will have billed Medicare Part B for their rescue and ambulance services and been paid $420.64 for the transport they provided to the first hospital emergency room. They were most likely on the scene of the accident for at least an hour, possibly longer with an ambulance and at least one engine as well. The personnel needed to accomplish our patient's initial rescue were numerous and the vehicles and equipment used were extremely sophisticated. I have no idea what they billed, but I do know how much they were paid for their ambulance services. That $420.64 is the standard fee for the level of service provided by the fire department as determined by the Center for Medicare and Medicaid Services (CMS or the Feds). The second ambulance transport, from one hospital to another moved up a pay grade to the maximum allowable ambulance fee available because of its medical complexity, and the payment schedule allowed us to collect a maximum amount of $719.52 for our services and equipment. That reimbursement would not cover my costs if I sent out two standard first aid providers to drag the patient down the block on a sled! But wait, this is how it works. The Feds will **allow** $719.52 but they're not going to pay that much. Remember, this is Medicare Part B coverage so they're only going to pay $80% of the cost they allowed. The Feds will only pay $575.61. Remember, there is no end to the 20% patient copay. It's a permanent patient assignment. The unpaid 20% difference of $143.90 is the patient's share of the payment. If the patient has purchased a second policy it will most likely pay the 20% that Medicare allowed but did not pay. If the patient has Public Aid backup, that balance of $143.90 won't be paid at all and the $575.61 will be the only money the ambulance company will ever get. The bill for our trauma patient was very high. It priced out at $5500.00. Now that's truly ghastly and I would be the first in line to admit it. But remember, I bill what I must in order to stay in business. Most fees for similar services in my geographic region by other companies are even higher than this. These are high end EMS services; designer EMS if you will. If the patient had private insurance, most of the costs would have been paid. Since our patient was a Medicare recipient, payment literally bottomed out. This patient's EOB would reflect the following information.

$575.61 (Amount paid) = $719.52 (the fee schedule rate) X 80%

$4780.48 (Provider write off) = $5500.00 (amount billed) - $719.52 (fee schedule rate)

The mandatory write off for this patient was $4780.48. The healthcare provider who accepts Medicare recipients as patients and contracts with the Feds to provide them with medical services can not collect any portion of the write off. Is it any wonder that more and more healthcare providers will not accept Medicare recipients as patients? If the Feds get their way, the fee schedule rates, which were already reduced at the beginning of this calendar year, will continue to decrease. We, in the healthcare industry, have no idea what planet our congress is living on. It most certainly is not mother earth.

In Chapter 3, we discussed Medicare funding, so by now, you should be an ace at this, right? The amount paid for all healthcare services provided to Medicare recipients is published by the Feds in the Physician's Fee Schedule. The Physicians Fee Schedule establishes rates for all healthcare provider reimbursements, not just physicians. It's that part of healthcare expenses that congress left out of Obamacare when they were figuring out how much healthcare was going to cost. I guess congress thinks the amount of money paid to healthcare providers does not qualify as part of the cost to provide healthcare. Perhaps Mr. Obama thought we were all going to work for free so there would be no need to put that expense into the cost analysis. If you are now lost by those comments, go back and read Chapter 3 again because you didn't get it the first time and it's important.

Public Aid EOBs:

Public Aid (or Medicaid) EOBs indicate the amount of money that the healthcare provider will be paid for their services if and when the States manage to come up with some money to pay their bills. That's not a snide comment. It's simple reality. I will not go into any long dissertation about Public Aid funding at this point, because most of what there is to say on this subject belongs under the fraud and abuse section of this book anyway. Large amounts of Pubic Aid funding have become nothing more than corruption. Suffice it to say that this area of healthcare infuriates most healthcare providers above all else. Public Aid recipients have no real interest in their EOBs because no matter what it says, in most cases they're not going to pay anyway. These EOBs can be extremely complicated or quite simple. It depends upon the system your State uses. In Illinois it is remarkably uncomplicated. Three lines does the job. In Indiana, the same explanation takes at least three pages. The amount that the healthcare provider has billed will be listed; then the amount that must be written off is subtracted, leaving a balance payable of about 6% to 10% of the bill. Each State sets its own fee schedule and payment system. If you're a Public Aid recipient, pay attention to this. If you change your residency to a different State, reapply for Public Aid funding in your new location or your bills will go unpaid and you may have to come up with the money yourself. If you live near the border between two States, consider applying for aid in both States if allowed. If not, you may need to pay for your own care and then apply to your State for reimbursement.

Some patients do not qualify for full Public Aid supported medical care. They have something called a "spend down". When their application is processed, they are told that they must pay a certain amount of money out of their own pocket before Public Aid will begin paying their bills. In theory, the patient keeps track of all of their bills, takes them to their Public Aid office where their case manager reviews them and assigns the amount of money they must pay out of their own pocket. The healthcare provider should get a copy of the spend down work sheet, but rarely ever does. Then, when the bills reach the preset spend down amount, Public Aid begins making payments. The Public Aid office does not check to see if the recipient has actually paid their bills. The patients provide the unpaid bills, get the financial assignment and then never bother to pay their primary assigned share. In the ten years I have been billing, I have been paid only once by a patient for their spend down share.

Most recipients of Public Aid couldn't care less who gets paid or whether or not anything is ever paid at all! They have all the information they need. They know they don't have to pay anything and they're not interested in how much the services actually cost. Many won't even provide their Public Aid numbers so their healthcare providers can file claims. They're totally disinterested. Even this wouldn't be so bad if we occasionally received a thank you. That very rarely happens. If anything, Public Aid recipients are more demanding and ungrateful than any other group of consumers in the healthcare mix. Public Aid is a fully socialized **entitlement** spending program and this group of consumers takes the definition of entitlement to a whole new level. By and large, they believe that their medical care is an inalienable right.

If our trauma patient had Public Aid as a pay source, the payment would have been $184.91 for the ambulance with an additional $2.70 per mile while the patient was on board the ambulance. That would be a grand total of $211.91 to cover the entire cost. The mandatory write off for this patient would have been $5288.09. Is it any wonder that fewer and fewer healthcare providers will accept Public Aid recipients as patients?

By now, the reader should have a very clear understanding of who is and who isn't paying for healthcare in this country. It certainly isn't the Federal government. More importantly, you should have figured out that the private insurance sector manages its resources well, while confusion, corruption and graft rein supreme in the federally controlled insurance arena. I told you right at the beginning of this book that the burdensome costs of healthcare are being carried on the backs of the working, taxpaying American Public. And yet, Nancy, Harry and Mr. Obama need more of your help. They want you to pay for another 17 million uninsured people. Or maybe that number has changed again. Who knows? What do you mean you can't do it? Are you one of those mean, nasty, selfish, conservative, right wing Republicans? Or, are you simply a level headed hard working, taxpaying American who knows that Obamacare is not going to work; is a disaster in the making? Let's scrap it altogether and get busy on a real solution so we can make some positive progress. Federal programs do not work. Medicare and Public Aid are abysmal failures.

Chapter 6
Our Military: Shameful Dirty Doings Then and Now.

We give very little to those whom we owe so much. It's appropriate that I sit at my desk today and work on this particular chapter in my book. It's Memorial Day weekend. On Memorial Day my employees have asked if they will be allowed to wear their "red shirts" on the ambulance instead of their required uniform shirts. In August of each year, I thank my employees with a picnic for them and their families where we eat, play games and have an all around good time sans alcohol. (I am a teetotaler; not to be confused with a tea bagger.) Traditionally, amongst other things, the company gives them a tee shirt which states 'We Support Our Troops" somewhere within a military or patriotic design theme. The colors and images change each year; however the support statement remains constant. Last year, the shirt was red with the raising of the American flag at Iwo Jima imprinted on the front. My employees are allowed to wear their shirts for one week after they're issued (there's a washer and dryer in their quarters to help avoid smelly situations) and thereafter upon request for special holidays such as the 4th of July. However, it's an all or nothing team effort. If one member of the team objects, they must all wear their regular uniform shirts. We have yet to have anyone object. My employees are a well blended mix of diverse backgrounds; race, religion, color and political affiliation. While I suspect that some may not support the wars we are engaged in, they still wholeheartedly support the troops who voluntarily risk their lives to protect us, and the principles of freedom we believe in. I find it gratifying that they spontaneously ask to be allowed to demonstrate their American spirit. I am saddened at the withdrawal of the Pledge of Allegiance from our schools. As a young child, I took great pride in standing up every day with my hand over my heart repeating the words I believe in so strongly.

Nothing could be more shameful than the manner in which we have handled the healthcare needs of our military personnel in the past. While we have made improvements in the conditions of our military hospitals over the years, nothing could have been more upsetting than the well publicized scandal over the shocking filth at Walter Reed Hospital in Bethesda, Maryland. It appears we still have a ways to go. Admittedly, the Federal Government cannot do it all. It takes help from the American people; people like Bill O'Reilly who consistently reminds us that we can all do a little something and who motivate us by example to do so. Whether you like the man or not, what ever the case may be, Bill O'Reilly is undeniably an American patriot; one who puts his money where his mouth is.

As a young child growing up in the late 1940's and early 1950's, I remember going to Hines VA hospital in Cook County, Illinois with my father. I have no memory of why we went or who we visited, but I clearly remember walking past row upon row of barracks-like buildings full of what I now know were World War II disabled veterans. When we entered the building my father had been looking for, I saw what appeared, in my childish eyes to be an endless row of occupied beds on each side of a long center isle with nothing more between them than a small cabinet on one side and a straight chair on the other; so close together that the occupants could have reached out to one another and touched hands. It was hot. It was noisy and the beds were full of permanently injured, crippled and disfigured men. I don't remember anything else about that visit. It is simply one of those vivid moments in time I think of as a "snapshot" image that for some unknown reason we carry with us throughout our lives.

As a young adult (a long time ago) working in the healthcare profession, I ended up back at Hines Hospital as an instructor for healthcare students who were going through a clinical rotation as part of their college course requirements. The barracks were closed by then; the occupants long ago moved on to other locations or buried in graves with stark white military markers; oddly impressive in their austere simplicity. The multi-storied main hospital was certainly a far cry from the barracks that housed our wounded veterans in the distant past of my childhood, but it was still noisy, smelly, dirty and badly overcrowded with nowhere near enough hospital staff to meet the needs of the patients. Those patients who were mobile often helped their fellow inmates who were too feeble to help themselves by feeding and assisting with changing their personal linens; one veteran helping another as is common in this unique brotherhood.

By no means was that the worst problem in a bad situation. At that time, no patient, veteran or otherwise had any meaningful say about, or input into the care they received in a hospital. If something needed to be done, the doctor ordered it and the staff made it happen insofar as was possible. Healthcare at that time in our past was a simpler, less technologically driven industry and was far more unsophisticated than it is now. Patients had no statutory rights in any hospital and trusted their doctors implicitly. Malpractice lawsuits were quite rare. For the most part, it worked reasonably well for it's time and in it's place with the exception of the VA system. Our military veterans were systematically under cared for and used like guinea pigs to produce research data without their permission or, in many cases, their knowledge. One such situation came to my (and my student's) attention which simply could not be silently tolerated. Not by me, at any rate and I lost my teaching position for being vocal about my objections. My team of six students had worked diligently with a patient through the course of his VA hospital stay of several weeks with great success and our patient was scheduled to be discharged over the impending weekend when my students and I would not be in the hospital for clinical work. On the following Monday, we arrived at the hospital and found our patient in the intensive care unit, comatose and on full life support where he died a few days later.

What happened? Just hours before our patient was scheduled to be discharged, one of several research teams composed of military medical staff physicians decided they needed further clinical data that could only be obtained by inserting an invasive monitoring line into his chest. Our patient was going home. There was no medical benefit or necessity for such a procedure. It was being done strictly for research purposes. In the process of performing the procedure, something went drastically wrong and our patient experienced a catastrophic stroke. What ever happened to "first do no harm"? I was outraged and my students were devastated. They had formed an affectionate bond with their patient and were proud of the successful results of their hard work. I hunted down the physician who had performed the procedure and informed him in no uncertain terms that he had no right to do such a thing; that what he had done was inhuman, unethical, immoral and he should never be allowed to practice medicine again. I wasn't whispering.

I immediately found out that the physician did indeed have the right to do exactly what he had done to our patient; or for that matter to any other patient in a VA hospital at will. I was informed that once patients entered into a VA healthcare setting, in exchange for their free healthcare, they waived any right to control the events of their care and personal medical information could be used indiscriminately; all in the name of research. In short, military patients could be used as guinea pigs for experimental research purposes without further written or verbal consent. The egregious manner in which this was conducted was supposedly offset by the benefits of future lives that might be saved through advances in medical knowledge and technology. This was a widespread acceptable practice throughout the VA medical system. My experience was not an isolated one.

Obviously, I lost my job on the spot, which is exactly what I expected to happen when I set out to ambush the doctor whom I believed to be responsible for my patient's untimely death. But I like to think that I, as well as many others like me had a tiny part in changing such an abhorrent practice simply by stating the obvious for all to hear. A few years later, many VA hospitals lost their research grants and Hines was one of many to do so. Such abominable practices have long since been abandoned and are, for the most part nothing more than a dim memory in the minds of some of our elder healthcare providers of which I am one.

Years later, I came across one of my Hines VA students who reminded me of that unfortunate episode and told me that her experience that day had been the single most important learning event in her educational process; that I had taught her what it meant to be a healthcare provider and a patient advocate. From that day forward, she had never lost her perspective and never questioned why she was in the healthcare industry. I guess my job was not lost in vain.

Our modern day VA hospital system, now for the most part keeps pace with the rest of the private and university based hospital systems. I like to believe that the Walter Reed scandal was an isolated occurrence which will not be repeated elsewhere. VA hospitals in Chicago and the surrounding Tri-state area; ones that I am familiar with, appear at least on the surface, not to be infected with the same deterioration in care and conditions as was Walter Reed. They deliver dedicated competent and compassionate care, but continue to be badly overcrowded at times and consistently unable to pay their bills in a timely manner. This is a Federal system and as such, they experience some of the same fraud, waste and abuse that's epidemic in all Federally controlled healthcare and entitlement initiatives. Additionally, the people who work in the VA systems are primarily civil service employees; some of whom have been known from time to time to be less than stellar in their performances. Certainly, all civil service employees are not slothful, but those who are, will most likely continue their lackadaisical performance until their retirement since it's nearly impossible to fire a civil service employee.

Our veteran military personnel who are chronically ill and unable to care for themselves have access to Federally funded healthcare benefits, however, they have enormous problems trying to access private sector healthcare providers. The reimbursement for this type of care is so small that most healthcare providers simply cannot afford to render the care that our disabled veterans need. The Federal government is faced with the overwhelming task of finding long term care settings for this group of veterans. In the event that our veterans are unable to obtain the care that they need directly from a military hospital, clinic or other care facility, they are sometimes faced with accepting care in some of the worst private healthcare centers imaginable. Should those centers be shut down? Of course they should, but they are very adept at barely meeting the requirements to remain open. They are cited for violations during inspection, clean up their act in time for a re-inspection and when they have passed, go back to their old ways. Multiple patients are packed into rooms that are too small, the bathrooms reek and the place may well be full of bugs. One place in particular is so bad that my ambulance crews try to touch as little as possible while in the facility and will not even go into a bathroom to wash their hands before they leave. They clean up in the ambulance with an alcohol gel solution after they have completed their episode of care. Not all extended care facilities with space set aside for our veterans are that bad but they are definitely a no frills extended care setting.

Why are they so substandard? The Federal government contracts with private care facilities to house these dependent veterans. The rate of reimbursement is so low, it is virtually impossible to attract a reasonably decent care center into the provider loop. Only those centers that cannot keep their beds full are attracted to the Federal system. Once again, it's all about money. It's about the business. In less populated areas, the situation is nowhere near as dire, but large cities have numerous care centers you wouldn't dream of placing your family members in. The Feds have to warehouse their debilitated veterans somewhere and it's going to end up being at the bottom of the healthcare facility barrel because the money just isn't there.

Active Military Personnel Insurance Coverage:

Civilian, non-military federal employees will be the first to tell you they have great healthcare insurance with very minimal out of pocket expense. Our congress, as well as many other Federal employees get free healthcare for life without paying anything out of pocket. Taxpayers are picking up the cost. Our active military, on the other hand must pay for their insurance just like the rest of us, only they're not paid anywhere near the salary they could earn in a non-military job of similar description. They're paid a pittance compared to non-military wage earners with similarly hazardous duties and their insurance coverage is extremely poor. Aren't they Federal employees?

Their insurance premiums and healthcare claims are handled by private insurance companies with government contracts. For example,

Tricare, managed by Humana is one of several insurance groups with an arrangement through the Federal government. Military insurance is controlled by the Feds, and is privatized much like Medicare Part C replacement policies. That's one of the few good things that can actually be said about military employee insurance. It's privatized so it's very carefully monitored by the private insurer. Private insurance companies don't handle these funds out of the goodness of their little black hearts. There's a profit in it for them. There's really nothing wrong with that. They're in business to make money and I'm fine with that. However, the amount paid to the healthcare provider is so substandard that very few private healthcare providers can sustain the losses they incur if they render healthcare to our military members and their families at the government fee for service rates. If active military personnel and their families are not able to obtain care at a nearby military base or affiliated healthcare center, they'll end up paying out of their own pockets and filing for reimbursement later from their government sponsored insurance company. They'll only get reimbursed a small percentage of the money they spent out of their own pockets for healthcare services. Something is backward here. Shouldn't the military be getting the really good insurance and congress be getting the cheap stuff? Shouldn't congress be paying out of their own pockets? To the best of my knowledge, only one congressman was reportedly shot at last year; or rather his office was and none of them had any limbs blown off.

Retired Military Personnel Insurance Coverage:

When military personnel retire or leave the service, they can continue to insure through their military policy. Most don't do that. In a perfect case scenario, our young people serve this country for their allotted time, leave the military in good standing and become part of the productive domestic work force in one capacity or another. When they enter the domestic work force, they generally opt for insurance provided by their employer. Why don't they keep their military insurance? They don't keep it because private insurance coverage will provide better benefits and far more access to care for themselves and their families. By and large, healthcare providers will not accept military insurance as a source of payment because the Feds won't allocate payment at a reasonable rate of reimbursement. It's that simple.

Permanently Disabled Military Personnel Insurance Coverage:

When the case scenario is not so perfect, and our young military people come home wounded and damaged, they're taken care of in a military hospital or a private facility which has contracted with the Feds to render their care. Over the years, the ability of our Veterans Administration (VA) system to provide their medical care has markedly improved and in many cases such as limb reconstruction they are on the cutting edge of medical technology; however, many of our wounded must still receive some of their services through non-military healthcare providers. These services are directly paid for by the Feds through the VA system.

Until recently, my company accepted payment for these services at the VA rate of reimbursement and the veteran was not billed for the balance as is required by Federal Law. Healthcare services were generally paid for at Medicare rates. When any healthcare provider cashes a VA check they are accepting the amount of money paid by the Feds as payment in full for the services rendered. Suddenly, without warning or explanation, our local VA system dropped the reimbursement rate of payment for non-contracted healthcare providers to the same amount of money that's paid by Public Aid for similar services. If you have forgotten, that's about six cents on the dollar. When we received the first such check, we called the VA system and asked why the check was below Medicare rates; a decrease of more than 30% in most cases. They were polite and apologetic in their noncommittal response. The reimbursement rates were dropped simply because they can do so at will. There was no explanation given. The uncashed check was sent back to the VA system with a letter explaining that we were unable to provide services to veterans at Public Aid rates and unfortunately, the patient would have to pay for his services out of his own pocket and then seek reimbursement through the VA system: a lengthy process at best. We have received several more checks for services rendered to veterans and paid at Public Aid rates which have also been left uncashed and returned to the VA. This is a sad event.

I don't think it's too difficult to figure out what's going on here. If the Feds continue to pay at a reduced rate, and the healthcare providers accept the payment, they save money. But the Feds know that in most cases that's not going to happen. The healthcare providers will either cease to provide care to the veterans at all or bill them directly for services rendered rather than billing the VA. The Feds are simply shifting the burden of payment onto the backs of our veterans. Once again, we see the Federal government controlling a healthcare product by manipulating the reimbursement rate downward. The result, of course is further rationing of the product; fewer healthcare providers willing to accept VA system patients. Well, Mr. Obama did say that we could reduce the cost of healthcare didn't he? Once their healthcare has been de-funded, we can give our veterans one of those wonderfully sensitive booklets produced by the Federal government that alludes to their lack of meaningful productivity and suggests what a burden they have become to their families, the healthcare system and society in general. Lovely!

Chapter 7
Your Not So Ordinary Dry As Dust Statistics; An Eye Opener?

In the course of everyday business, my employees produce medical records documenting all aspects of care that our patients have received during their ambulance transports. In addition to medical information, we collect and document various demographic details which may be useful in enabling us to understand the nature of our business. Understanding the nature of any business is key to being able to identify shifting demands, predict what resources will be needed and in general remain cost effective. All of this information is entered into a computer data system which allows us to generate statistical reports. Working with systems such as this can be tricky. Data can be skewed and results inaccurate if the system does not hold useful information or the reports generated do not take into consideration the correct data. In other words, garbage in is equal to garbage out.

I created my own system of data gathering and reporting rather than purchase existing software for two reasons. I'm too cheap to pay an exorbitant price for something I can do myself and I wanted to make certain that the data going into and coming out of the system is not skewed by omissions and inaccuracies. I don't want garbage out. If this type of system is used appropriately, we can determine the average age of our patients, their sex, race, religion, pay source, primary diagnosis, past medical history and analyze anything else we decide we need to track in order to take a closer look. This information helps us shift resources, maximize productivity, minimize costs and most importantly predict and provide for changing trends in the marketplace. Once we collect all appropriate information, the system data can be analyzed by producing reports which give us numbers or percentages using specific qualifiers.

For instance, we can determine what percentage of our patient population was male and what percentage was female over a given period of time. In fact, if we add to our report definition we can find out how many patients under the age of 40 years were male. We can continue to qualify (or filter) our data to tell us what percentage of our patient population was African American, male, below the age of 40 years, transported between the hours of midnight and 6AM, having a heart attack and was privately insured. If you collect the right kind of information into your system, it can produce insightful and invaluable information.

The reports produced for this chapter, cover all levels of ambulance service provided over a span of one year; the last eight months of the year 2009 and the first 4 months of the year 2010. The total number of patients transported during this time period was 2,374. The first set of numbers represents the total number of patients transported in each pay source category, the percentage of the overall volume of business and the average amount per dollar billed that we actually collected. The second set of numbers break out the pay sources by the ethnic origin of the patients, lists the total number of patients transported for that group and what percentage that is of the total ethnic group. As you can see from the data, less than one third of our patient population had private insurance. If the Feds are unhappy with the state of affairs in the insurance industry, they have no one to blame but themselves since they are providing the lions share of insurance coverage in this country. I offer no analysis, qualifiers, explanations or excuses. The numbers are what they are and I can assure you there was no garbage going in.

Pay Source	Total # of Patients	% Of Total Volume	Average Payment
Private Insurance	689	29%	.75/1.00
Medicare	799	34%	.35/1.00
Public Aid	606	26%	.06/1.00
None	212	08%	.00/1.00
Military	68	03%	.40/1.00

Ethnic Group	Total #/%	Insurance	Medicare	Public Aid	None	Other
African American	478/20%	85/18%	142/30%	185/39%	57/12%	9/01%
Caucasian	1290/54%	481/37%	558/43%	142/11%	63/04%	46/05%
Hispanic	438/30%	121/30%	32/07%	220/50%	59/13%	6/0%
All Other	168/07%	53/32%	41/25%	50/30%	18/11%	6/2%

Only 29% of our patient population had private healthcare insurance. Privately insured patients throughout the country are paying the lion's share of healthcare costs for the entire nation.

Chapter 8

Fraud and Abuse: The Real Down and Dirty Behind The Scenes Corruption; Who Are Some Of The Really Bad Guys?

Unfortunately, fraud and abuse are rampant, out of control problems in the healthcare industry; therefore this is going to be a lengthy chapter. Each of the three major healthcare industry pay sources are represented; private insurance, Medicare and Public Aid as well as fraud and abuse initiated by patients and providers. Fraud and abuse are daily occurrences in the healthcare setting and cost the taxpayers and individual patients enormous sums of money. The cases listed in this chapter don't even scratch the surface of this overwhelming problem.

For instance, yesterday, when I opened the company mail two payments we received from major healthcare insurance companies had creatively manipulated reimbursement amounts. The insurance companies had managed to shift most of the responsibility for payment over to the patients. One check was from United Healthcare and the other from Aetna. Both cited fee schedules, non-covered expenses and out of network provider services as an excuse for low payments. Both checks covered emergent transports which should have been paid at a much higher rate. Patients are relieved of all financial penalties for not using a PPO provider in emergent situations. What's really amazing is both companies are co-defendants in a current class action lawsuit and are being sued for price fixing when paying out of network providers. United Healthcare has settled out of court. It remains to be seen, what Aetna will do. One thing is certain; the penalties being levied against these insurance companies are obviously not high enough to deter the activity. Price fixing remains a lucrative practice in spite of millions of dollars in damages being paid out by insurance companies in numerous class action lawsuits. Insurance companies can afford to pay millions of dollars in damages when illegal activities bring in billions of dollars in income. The United Healthcare (and Aetna) lawsuit is discussed further on in this chapter.

Private Insurance Fraud:

Humana, one of the largest insurance companies in this country has managed to attract a very large number of class action lawsuits. However, few of their suits ever go to trial. They generally settle the suit before trial for an amount of money far less than would most likely be awarded by the court should the case go to trial and the plaintiffs win. The amount that Humana settles their law suits for, including legal fees is generally far less than they were able to net the company with their questionable practices. Most large insurance companies simply view the payment of lawsuits as part of the cost of doing business. In most cases, these practices are aimed directly at non-PPO providers who will not contract at substandard rates with the insurance company for their services. Humana keeps its cost of doing business down at the expense of the healthcare providers and the patients until such time as they are sued and forced to clean up their act. Once the suit is settled, they simply find another way to manipulate the system. I would suggest that the interested reader research this subject on the internet by typing "Human class action law suits" into their internet browser bar. These legal actions are a matter of public record. Despite the large amounts of money paid to the plaintiffs in these lawsuits, the payment amount is a drop in the bucket compared to what Humana netted over time with these activities. One issue that consistently comes up in these law suits is below market rate payments of legitimate medical claims resulting in reduced payments to the healthcare providers who pass the unpaid balances on to the patients. They engage in price fixing by using payment schedules which list below par rates of reimbursement for specific medical procedures and services. This practice spans many years and has netted the company huge volumes of money for claims that are paid at substandard rates leaving the patients and healthcare providers responsible for the shortfall funds. When these law suits are settled, the amount that's paid out in penalties and legal fees by Humana is far less than the actual losses experienced by the healthcare providers and patients.

From a financial standpoint, this may not be a bad business strategy. For instance, let's say Humana withheld $250 million in legitimate claims and then settled for a payout of $100 million to the class action group. They still net a terrific profit of $150 million. This practice has been going on for years and will most likely continue in one variation or another simply because it's profitable. Despite the fact that insurance companies have to pay out millions of dollars in damages, they still net a sizable amount of money over the long run. These problems will not go away if the legal defense costs plus payable proceeds of the lawsuits do not penalize the insurer at a cost greater than the amount that the company was able to net with the proceeds of their crime. This is an easy fix. First, eliminate the questionable PPO system altogether. If the PPO system didn't exist, then none of the questionable practices associated with that system would have a breeding ground to flourish in. Instead of trying to regulate a system that breeds corruption, simply abolish the practice. Then hold the insurance company liable for 110% of the actual proceeds they were able to net from their illegal activity as well as their court costs. If penalties were assessed at realistically punitive levels, the insurance companies might not be quite so quick to engage in this type of activity. While Humana is one of the largest insurance companies engaging in these activities, they are, by no means the only ones to do so.

Another way for an insurance company to save money is to make certain that their insured clients; the insurance policy holders are cared for in PPO or preferred provider hospitals. One particular **private insurance company** has a very large network and will go to great lengths, more so than any other insurance company to make certain anyone with their insurance does not receive care in an out of network hospital. They can only be described as fanatical in their activities to get patients into their own network system. There is no problem with this practice if the patient has a prescheduled medical or surgical issue. And it most certainly is fine for routine out of hospital exams and testing. Theoretically, it saves everyone money.

What about an emergent event? When someone has a life threatening emergency, the fire department takes the patient to the nearest hospital. They are not concerned with anything other than saving the patients life as is appropriate. Most insurance companies accept this as an unavoidable financial event and cover the patient's medical expenses according to the terms of the patient's policy even though they are in an "out of network" situation. In an emergency, most insurance companies relieve patients of PPO policy restrictions. They are certainly not going to insist that a patient who is in the middle of having a heart attack be transferred by ambulance to another hospital in order to pursue a PPO discount; that is, with the exception of our unnamed insurance company. They will do precisely that! This particular unnamed insurance company carries this activity to such an extreme that patients, at times are medically jeopardized.

I hold, in my possession a large number of original patient charts which consistently state that the patient is being transferred at the request of the insurance company. Each of these charts clearly document that the patient was being transferred from a non participating hospital into a PPO hospital. In each instance, there was no clear medical advantage for the patient and a large number of these patients were critically ill, being cared for in intensive care units and were in no condition to be transferred. Ambulance transports are not without risks! No patient should be transferred solely for the sake of obtaining a discount when they are critically ill! How many of these patients, lying flat on their backs, terrified and in pain, were told that they had to be transferred or their insurance company would not pay their bills? If the patient is stable and all parties (patient, sending hospital and receiving hospital) agree to the transfer, that's fine. They're all on the same page and the transport risk is minimized when the patient is stable. When those favorable circumstances do not exist, the wellbeing of those patients should never be compromised for the sake of a PPO discount.

To the best of my knowledge, there is only one insurance company that does this on a regular, daily basis. In a ten year history of ambulance transport services, my company has never been asked to transfer a critically ill patient to obtain a PPO discount by any other insurance carrier. The name of this insurance company has been left out because this information is not public knowledge despite the fact that this activity happens on a daily, perhaps hourly, basis. This same insurance company has standing PPO ambulance companies who have no qualms about moving patients around from hospital to hospital for the financial advantage of the insurer and themselves. They do a brisk and profitable business by engaging in these transports.

If you or any of your family members have been literally forced to move from one hospital to another when critically ill in order to remain within your insurance network, you already know who this company is. What can you do about it? First of all, make certain that the transport was, beyond all shadow of a doubt done solely in order to move the patient into a PPO network, that the patient was critically ill and that the patient (or family of the patient) was told that the insurance company would not pay for healthcare services where they were at. The circumstances need to be obvious. Then report it to your State Insurance Board and ask them specifically who you should report this behavior to in your respective States. Some States differ from others in handling these types of problems. In some instances, you could end up talking to the Office of the Inspector General.

If your family member actually died, or was seriously medically compromised during such a transport due to the delay of care which results in situations such as this, seek the advice of a competent lawyer. I abhor frivolous law suits in the medical industry because they are part of the huge cost of providing healthcare, but this is an example of real abuse on the part of both the insurance company and the transport company who agreed to move a critically ill patient into a PPO hospital when there was no medical advantage to be obtained. If the patient was critically ill and transferred for a clear medical advantage then the fact that they were transferred into a network hospital is of no consequence as long as the receiving hospital could provide a higher level of care. If the patient or their family requested the transfer in order to remain in the care of their PPO medical group despite the critical nature of the event, then there is also no abuse of the system. The transfer of a critically ill patient is always dangerous but sometimes necessary to obtain more sophisticated medical care. However, the transfer of a critically ill patient should never be done without a clear medical advantage. This dangerous and manipulative practice will only stop if the victims and their families speak out. My company's attempts to correct this practice were met with a complete lack of interest when we filed a complaint against this unnamed insurance company.

United Healthcare, Aetna and Cigna are tied for second place in the financial scams division of the private insurance company fraud and abuse contest. Once again, the internet is your best source of information. Type the words "ingenix/ucr class actions" in your internet browser. Pay attention to the New Jersey courts and you'll find lots of interesting information pertaining to class action suits naming multiple insurance companies; insurers whose names are very familiar and who have consistently engaged in price fixing, substandard practices and a host of other shady activities all in the name of the almighty profit. United Healthcare has agreed to settle for $350 million dollars in damages for price fixing. Aetna and Cigna were also named in the same suit. Their positions are yet to be clarified in this action.

In Chapter 2, insurance terms were defined, and amongst those terms was the phrase "usual and customary". You were informed that private insurance companies wormed their way out of legitimate claims by stating that a billed service was above usual and customary. Then the healthcare providers and patients were stuck with the unpaid balances. This class action lawsuit addresses that issue. Once again, the problem exists in the PPO sector of the insurance industry. Price fixing is a repetitive theme in lawsuits involving private healthcare insurance companies who specifically target non-PPO providers.

United Healthcare is the parent company for a subsidiary or sister company named Ingenix. Ingenix was established solely to set reimbursement rates for all medical goods and services. Then that rate information or fee schedule was sold to various other insurance companies. Follow me so far? Ingenix, who was owned by United Healthcare developed a database of average charges for any given medical service and then published the rates as "usual and customary". Aetna contributed large volumes of data to Ingenix and then all three of the above named insurance companies used this "fee schedule" to limit the amount of money they paid to healthcare providers for any and all medical goods and services. Not all healthcare providers were affected, just the non-par, or non PPO providers. The PPO providers were already under contract for set fees so the usual and customary fee schedule did not apply to them. There was only one problem with this system. Ingenix/United Healthcare cooked the numbers in order to fix prices at a rate below market value, which is illegal. This is a database system. Remember; garbage in, garbage out? The non-PPO healthcare providers passed the unpaid balances on to the patients. Some patients paid and some didn't. This scam went on for more than 10 years and countless healthcare providers as well as patients were financially damaged. Is $350 million dollars enough? United Healthcare most certainly netted vastly higher sums over the course of years that this activity was carried out, so the punishment does not fit the crime. There is no real deterrent to keep any insurance company from coming up with a new scam to increase their profit margins whenever they can net a substantial amount of money above and beyond the amount of their penalty. Once again, the corruption was centered around the PPO system of claim payments. Any system that breeds this amount of corruption should be eliminated.

Third party negotiators are another group that should be watched carefully. They're not providers of healthcare. They're insurance company collaborators. They fall into the same category as billing and payroll service companies which are opportunistic byproducts of the main industry. Years ago, an enterprising group of business people came up with a terrific idea to make money without really working very hard for it. In fact, it was brilliant; it worked exceedingly well and is in common use today.

They simply formed an independent, stand alone company and inserted themselves between the insurance companies and the healthcare providers. These companies deal almost exclusively with non-PPO healthcare providers who do not have a reduced fee contract in place with the insurer. Their purpose is to negotiate with the healthcare provider to obtain a discount for the insurance company on the total dollar amount of the healthcare providers claim for services. The negotiators then receive a percentage of the negotiated savings. This is a win win situation for the insurance company and the negotiators. If a patient decides to use a non-PPO healthcare provider in a non-emergent situation, they already know that they're going to pay a larger share of the cost. However, in an emergency, that's not the case. We don't stand around and discuss the pay source or call the insurance company for permission to use a non-PPO healthcare provider in an emergency situation. Insurance companies must pay the higher fee as if the service had been provided by a contracted service group. At the present time, when insurance companies receive emergency service bills from non-PPO providers, many turn those bills over to these negotiators.

What about the healthcare providers and the patients? How do they fare in these negotiations? Well, the provider gets paid in two weeks if they have accepted the lower negotiated rate. They accept the reduction in the payment amount in order to get cash in hand quickly. The patient gets to pay their copay, deductible and non covered services just as usual. Rarely is there a benefit for the patient.

Several years ago, we naively entered into an agreement with one of these negotiation companies. They represented roughly ten different small, self funded insurance groups and were actually a reasonably straightforward group of people to do business with. We gave them an across the board 20% discount with one stipulation. The patient could not be assigned any financial obligations for deductibles, copays or not covered services. The insurance company and negotiator could divvy up the 20% as they pleased. We were willing to take the 20% hit in return for a two week turnaround on payments, and the patient, negotiator and insurance company all got something positive out of the arrangement. The whole thing worked well all the way around until **MultiPlan** took over our nice little group.

MultiPlan entered us into discount agreements with hundreds of insurance companies without our knowledge. Suddenly, nearly every insurance company we billed sent reduced checks for "MultiPlan" discounts; many with as much as 40% to 60% reductions in payments. Not only did they take a huge bite out of our billed charges, they assigned the patient their copays, deductibles and non-covered expenses. Suddenly, the financial advantage shifted solely to the insurance company and MultiPlan. When we tried to cancel our agreement, our requests were ignored or lost track of for at least six months. It took us nearly two years to straighten out our accounts receivables and get MultiPlan out of the picture. To this day, we still receive fax transmittals requesting that we accept a 40 to 60% reduction in the payment of our fees on a case by case basis. These offers still continue to be misleading and, if accepted would still end up costing the healthcare provider and patient a large amount of money while the insurer and Multiplan would pocket a nice profit. This is not illegal, just underhanded and sneaky. Yesterday, our fax machine coughed out an offer from MultiPlan requesting a 66% discount. The patient would still have been responsible for their deductible, copay and not covered expenses.

Let's look at another transport ambulance bill for $3000.00. Multiplan will offer to pay about $1800.00. Then, in the fine print of this mini-contract it says "minus not covered services, copays, and deductibles" which the healthcare provider can collect from the patient. The only thing the patient does not have to pay is the original 40% discount that MultiPlan is requesting on the total billed amount of the claim. In fact, by the time the bill is paid, the $3000.00 has been reduced by the $1200.00 discount, the patient's copay, the patient's deductible and the not covered services. The actual check will most likely be $600.00 or less. All offers such as this are rejected and the insurance company theoretically pays based on the patients policy. When the patient gets a bill from us, they are understandably floored. To add insult to injury, some of our patients have called their insurance companies and complained that they have not paid enough of our bill and that they are stuck with a large balance. The insurance company has the nerve to tell the patient that the reason their bill is so large is that we refused to negotiate! Then we're left to explain that if we had negotiated, none of the discount the insurance company would have gotten would have been passed on to them. They would still have been stuck with the same amount to pay. Our response to MultiPlan is consistently the same. No thanks; we'll discount the patient when they call in with questions about their bills.

Another trick used by third party negotiators involves misrepresentation. Since many healthcare providers will not deal with third party negotiators, they call the healthcare provider's office and state that they are calling about an insurance bill for services rendered to Patient XYZ on a specific date of service giving the healthcare providers office the impression that they are speaking d**irectly** to an insurance company representative. They do not state that they are third party negotiators and not employees of the insurance company. Only when they are pressed with specific questions about their relationship with the insurance company does the healthcare provider find out that they have a third party negotiator on the line. I do, at times negotiate directly with self funded groups and give discounts that are favorable to all concerned as do other healthcare provider groups so it's very easy to get trapped in one of these situations. However, as they say "the devil is in the details". We soon figure out that there is no benefit to the patient and the conversation is quickly closed.

Private insurance company fraud will continue to blossom and thrive until the financial penalty is greater than the proceeds of the fraudulent activity. Since a large amount of this fraud centers around Preferred Provider Organization issues, a quick cure for the problem would be to eliminate the PPO practice in healthcare insurance altogether. As long as PPO provider policies exist in their current form, they will continue to attract corruption and manipulation on an enormous scale. While the providers certainly suffer financially under this system, the patients and their families are ultimately the ones to pay the highest price for this widespread abuse.

Why not just regulate the PPO system more closely? If the original concept turns out to be faulty and flawed, regulating it only does one thing. It opens up further avenues of abuse. Most of the time, the language that regulates one problem opens a new door to corruption somewhere else in the system. Then the next problem must be regulated. And, so forth and so on. If you have a faulty system and you want to correct the problem, get rid of what is at fault. Get rid of whatever is holding the door open to corruption.

Medicare Fraud:

The Medicare system is quite easily pillaged and plundered for large sums of money on a daily basis by corrupt healthcare providers. It's very simple to pull off and difficult to identify. The Federal government has never been able to control much of the abuse because the actual Medicare system is unbelievably convoluted and complicated. The more convoluted and regulated a system, the more difficult it is to track anything through it.

Most healthcare providers who are actually rendering care to patients, have no idea how the Medicare system works and are blissfully unaware that corruption exists. They're busy taking care of patients, not watching out for fraud. Other healthcare providers are aware of its existence but are hesitant to report it because they fear losing their jobs or have no idea how to go about reporting such a problem. And then there are the major scams where everyone involved in the patient's care is in on the deal.

Medicare scams are far easier to engage in than are private insurance scams. Beyond the fact that the Medicare system is too cumbersome to police itself, the major reason for the overabundance of fraudulent activity is very simple. Most privately insured patients are younger and less vulnerable to abuse than are Medicare patients. They can and do read their medical bills and are able to question the charges that are detailed in the billing statements sent to them by their insurance companies. It's far easier to prey upon the elderly, frail and oft times confused patient in a gigantic unwieldy federal system than it is a savvy youngster who has a medical bill to pay. How easy is it to scam the system? Let's take a look at a few examples.

My own encounter with a Medicare fraud case was not difficult to spot. Early in my ambulance transport career, the company I worked for had an unusually large number of transports from one single extended care facility into Weis Hospital in Chicago. The extended care facility (long since extinct) was literally, around the corner and down the block from the Hospital. The patients were nearly all very elderly and at best, confused. Most were seriously debilitated and many were comatose with life support systems in use such as mechanical ventilators. Almost every afternoon, day in and day out, we were called to transfer patients around the corner In to the Weis Hospital emergency room. Well, given the ages and medical conditions of the patients, this was not necessarily something to be unduly concerned about. It is, in fact quite common for very frequent, legitimate transports to take place in an elderly patient population with such a large number of complicated medical problems.

However, on the day that I was scheduled to take three patients, one after another from the nursing home to the hospital, what had been a growing sense of unease on my part became fully alarming. For payment of all Medicare patient ambulance transports, there must be a valid documented reason for the transport to take place. All three patients were diagnosed with chest pain. After transporting the first two patients, we evaluated the last for transfer. The third patient was fully comatose and unable to respond in any way; no blinking, squeezing hands or responses to pain were noted and he had been in this condition for weeks. How could this patient have communicated a sense of pain to anyone? I assumed I had the wrong patient and went to check at the nursing station where I was assured that I did indeed have the correct patient. I wisely kept my mouth shut, completed the patient's transport and then contacted the Office of the Inspector General where the circumstances of this event were duly noted by them. Nothing happened. The ambulance transports continued for a considerable length of time. Then one day, out of the clear blue sky, a major Medicare scandal hit the front pages of the Chicago newspapers. The nursing home culprits had been nabbed. There had been a series of reports to the Feds about possible Medicare abuses in the same nursing home that I had reported on previously. They had been under investigation for quite some time.

The physician who had ordered all the ambulance transports owned the nursing home and was also on staff at Weiss Hospital. When one of his patients was running out of payable Medicare days, the physician would simply come up with a new subjective medical problem and have his patients transferred into the hospital where he would then bill for their medical care. In the case I reported, the physician simply got sloppy and used a transfer diagnosis which was not believable given the patient's condition. These patients remained in the hospital for three days in the care of the same physician who had ordered their transfer. Then they were transported back to the nursing home with their Medicare days renewed for another round of Federally funded payments. Obviously, this took a lot of cooperation on the part of the nursing and caregiver staff. This scam went on for several years and cost the taxpayers huge sums of money.

The Federal system would never have picked this fraud up if observant healthcare providers didn't report the suspicious activity. You have to wonder how much of this type of activity has gone undetected over the years and how much continues in some variant form today. A private insurance company would have picked up a problem of this magnitude very quickly. Their systems of fraud detection are far more efficient. Of course these problems were further regulated out of existence, right? New methods to monitor this activity were put into place; therefore, the manner in which this type of scam is conducted has simply altered to adjust to the new monitoring systems. The problem will continue to exist until the ridiculous medigap system which opens the door to this abuse is eliminated. It's the system that invites corruption and breeds abuse. Change the system.

Another interesting case involved Doctor's Hospital in Hyde Park on the south side of Chicago. There were so many illegal activities in that hospital, it's hard to believe there could have been enough time left for legitimate healthcare practices to take place.

The neighborhood surrounding the hospital had a very high concentration of homeless persons as well as drug addicts, pimps and prostitutes. "Messengers" from the hospital were sent into the streets with cash in hand to entice addicts and homeless people into becoming patients in the hospital. They were admitted through the emergency room and then "housed" for a considerable length of time; many for extended visits. The physicians who were involved in this scam created false records documenting medical care and visits, procedures, testing and laboratory results for their guests and then proceeded to bill the appropriate Federally funded programs for these imaginary services. Their guests were no longer homeless; at least temporarily, and were safe, warm, dry and well fed. They entered and left the hospital at will, much like a hotel. Obviously, fraud of this magnitude required a great deal of cooperation on the part of the hospital staff. The fines for this fraud, once it was exposed, were so severe that the hospital was unable to financially recover and was compelled to close its doors in the year 2000. Heavy fines amounting to approximately 20 million dollars were levied against the primary culprits in this scheme and some jail time was handed out. However, it is unlikely that the total amount of the fines ever constituted anything close to full repayment of misused funds back to the Federal government; or should I say, back to the taxpayers. Had our culprits kept this on a small scale, it might still be going on undetected today with no one the wiser. Perhaps it still is.

Our last example of physician initiated fraud involved outpatient psychiatric care charges for patients housed as inpatients in psychiatric care facilities. These patients were not diagnostically severe enough to require full care in a hospital but were not emotionally and mentally stable enough to handle the stressful rigors of day to day life without supervised living conditions. The physician/owner of several such facilities loaded his patients onto a bus once a week and transported them to another site for group "psychiatric outpatient therapy". No therapy secessions ever actually took place. The patients simply sat around for an extended period of time waiting to be taken back to the care facility. The physician then billed for therapy secessions for each of these patients whom he had, in fact never seen.

In all these physician initiated Medicare fraud cases, the healthcare provider identified and targeted a specific type of patient population. All of these cases involved patients who would not be able or likely to blow any whistles. They were all either physically or psychologically impaired. This type of illegal activity is nearly impossible to stamp out without the help of the healthcare providers themselves.

Patients also become direct financial victims of the system. Most don't understand the complicated rules and regulations of the Medicare system and are therefore unable to protect themselves. A large ambulance company in the Chicago Metropolitan Area made the local TV news channels a few years ago because of their billing practices. The subject arose because a patient's family received bills for services that they thought were too costly. Despite an in depth report, the most important detail in the event was completely missed. It wasn't the size of the bills that constituted the major problem; it's the fact that bills existed at all. The patient was a Medicare recipient.

Ambulance transport bills are almost always very costly; most especially in the private sector. It is a simple fact that the private ambulance industry is the red-headed stepchild in the healthcare industry; largely ignored and consistently under funded by both State and Federal agencies. The amount billed to the patient for services in this particular case was the subject of the TV report, when in fact; the real issue was completely lost because very few people understand Medicare Part A and B billing criteria.

Ambulance companies constantly vie with one another for business. If their vehicles don't run, they're out of business very quickly. It's so unbelievably difficult to make ends meet in this industry that much of this competition is vicious and underhanded. That competition can and sometimes does lead very quickly to corruption, graft and bribery. Most private ambulance companies seek contracts with major hospitals to provide all of their transport services in order to secure their financial futures. Conversely, most hospitals seek contracts with ambulance carriers who are not going to cost them any money. Hospitals want ambulance companies to obtain their funds by billing private insurance, Medicare and Medicaid. For the most part, this works quite well for all concerned. Just ignore the fact that some of these contracts are obtained with the assistance of under the table gratuities to key hospital administrators. That's a whole different problem and not all hospitals or ambulance companies are guilty of that activity.

Medicare Part A pays for the patient's "in" hospital charges and the hospital must bill for those fees. Medicare Part B pays for the patient's "out" of hospital charges; therefore the ambulance company must bill for those fees. Seems pretty clear, right? If the patient is leaving the hospital then the ambulance company must do their own billing to the appropriate pay source. There is, of course, a grey area. If the patient does not remain out of the hospital for at least 72 hours, Medicare Part B will not pay the ambulance provider. The hospital that the patient was transported out of and then returned to **must** pay the ambulance company for the transport out of their own funds which they have obtained from Medicare Part A billing. Surprisingly enough, the Feds have this issue pretty well policed. The emphasis here is on the word must. If the ambulance company says, "Oh, don't worry about that, if we get all your business, we'll make certain you don't get billed for those transports. We'll just write them off.", they are engaging in a kickback agreement. A bribe, if you will. Most ambulance companies who engage in this type of activity are intelligent enough to just write the loss off and no one is the wiser; at least to the extent that the activity would not glaringly surface. Not so, our subject ambulance company. They turned around and billed the Medicare patient directly.

This particular patient was in a hospital that had a free standing MRI and radiation therapy center located on the campus about one quarter of a mile from the main hospital building. This is a very common setup which allows the hospital to provide services to both inpatient and outpatient clientele in a very efficient manner. In order to get this particular patient from the hospital to the outpatient center, he needed to be moved by an ambulance crew due to the debilitating nature of his illness. The crew picked up the patient, dropped him off at the outpatient center for his therapy and then returned later the same day to transport him back to his room in the main hospital when his care at the outpatient center had been completed. The patient had two ambulance transports per day on multiple occasions during the course of his hospital stay. Now, the ambulance company knew that they couldn't bill Medicare because the service was not payable based on the 72 hour rule. They also knew that if they billed the hospital as should have been done, they would endanger their contract. So, they billed the patient for multiple ambulance transports, who by Medicare regulations should never have seen a bill for any of these services at all.

More than one person who saw this news clip reported the abuse to the Center for Medicare and Medicaid Services. However, it's very unlikely that anything was ever done about it. If the situation had been carefully investigated, it would have lead to the exposure of large numbers of other similar graft and corruption cases in the industry and would have made it into the National news media. It never did. Why? I can only surmise that since Medicare wasn't directly defrauded of any funds, they weren't interested. It wasn't costing the Feds a penny; just the patient. It was the consumer who was the victim of fraud, not the Medicare system and as such seemed to be of little interest since it didn't cost Medicare any money. During the TV interview of the ambulance company spokesperson, the reporter only briefly touched on the subject of billing practices and when the question arose as to why Medicare was not billed, the answer was "it's complicated" and the issue was not pursued by the investigative reporter. I would be willing to bet that several ambulance companies and hospital administrators were holding their collective breaths for a long period of time, waiting to see if a full scale investigation was going to erupt. I'm not positive, but I believe that the patient's ambulance transport bills were written off.

These cases are just a small sample of the fraud and abuse that takes place in government supported healthcare systems. The more complicated and convoluted the rules, the more loopholes are opened up for abuse of the system. The less knowledge and control over their own healthcare issues that patients have, the easier it is to defraud them, or the system on their behalf. The 72 hour Medigap rule alone must surely cost far more money in fraudulent activities than it saves the government in non-payment of those same Medigap days. Nothing could be more complicated than Medicare regulations. Some abuse could be stopped quickly with more stringent controls in the existing system; however, a certain amount of fraud will always exist. It's easy money. Best solution? Privatize the system. The Feds have already screwed it up royally. It will be less complicated, more vigilantly watched and far less costly to run. Then, all we have to do is figure out how to keep the private insurance companies from steeling us blind. We should be able to do that with much higher financial penalties for corrupt behavior. Make certain that it isn't worth their while to try and scam the system.

There are some things we could do to stop at least a portion of Medicare abuse under its current structure. An organized campaign of Medicare fraud awareness would certainly eliminate a certain amount of these practices. Most healthcare providers have little or no understanding of how the Medicare system works or what to do if something occurs which they feel is questionable. Healthcare providers, for the most part are decent, hardworking people who would not engage in or condone such activities. They're aware that fraud is taking place but don't know exactly where, when or how it's happening. They're not trained to recognize it. Our nurses would be most likely to recognize abusive and fraudulent practices before anyone else in the system. If specific course curriculum designed to teach them how to identify fraud were included as required elements in their educational programs it would certainly help. Who better to identify this type of activity? After all, fraud can be identified in its early stages by signs and symptoms just as illnesses can. With a properly trained eye, we could weed out some of the corruption early on. All healthcare providers should receive specific detailed information during their educational years which teaches them to identify fraudulent activities and how to deal with them. They should be taught exactly what constitutes fraud in the healthcare setting.

All employers must post employment practice posters in prominent places throughout the workplace. Why not develop medical fraud and abuse posters which list specific activities to watch for and what to do in the event such an activity is observed or suspected. Mandate that this information be posted prominently throughout hospitals and care centers. Make certain these posters give instructions for reporting suspect occurrences and how to handle the situation; who to call, and give assurances that the caller will remain anonymous.

All healthcare facilities must annually in-service their employees in certain areas such as disease transmission, hand washing and a host of other subjects which are key areas of difficulty the healthcare community at large wishes to focus on. Hospitals can't retain their accreditation without covering these educational issues. Why not develop a short program dealing with this subject and include it in hospital continuing education requirements? Make it a requirement for continuing hospital accreditation.

Patients all receive explanation of benefit statements. When these statements are mailed to the patient, include the same information for them. Make sure that patients understand just how devastating fraudulent activity is to the financial future of their own healthcare system; that our ability to continue providing their care is dependent upon making sure that taxpayer funding is not wasted.

There needs to be a stepped up awareness of how to specifically identify fraudulent activity, not just abstract knowledge that it exists. We need to personalize that knowledge into a format that is meaningful to the individual and provide a fast track system to engage in an all out war against Medicare fraud. The Feds have known about this problem for years and have never been able to make even a tiny dent in the problem. Perhaps the best way to clean up the system is to privatize it. With a potential profit on the horizon for private insurance companies, many of the problems inherent in the federal system would decrease dramatically; in fact, almost overnight.

Medicaid or Public Aid Insurance:

No single handout provided by Federal and State government agencies causes as much resentment on the part of American taxpayers as does Public Aid. What was once considered a hand up during hard times has become a permanent hand out; a way of life for many people. They are lined up in droves for that free candy. Only it's certainly not free. I'm paying for it and so are you and I don't like it. Most working middle class Americans are sick to death of seeing their hard earned dollars support programs that foster greed, sloth and abuse on a monumental scale. Are some of the recipients of Public Aid worthy of our help and support? Certainly; there are many cases of families who would be destitute without supportive aid for a chronically ill child or other family member. There are a large number of needy cases worth supporting. Unfortunately, Public Aid funding is so easily obtained it's become a primary target for graft, greed and corruption in our society.

Recently, one of my employees arrived at work in a rage after having stood behind a woman at the grocery store checkout. He said he was sick and tired of watching someone check out with items such as steak and lobster tail, soda, candy, junk food and costly items he couldn't possibly afford to buy and then hand over a Public Aid card supported by his tax dollars instead of cash. He told the woman she should thank him because he just paid for her groceries and that he had a wife and three children to support and could not possibly afford to buy half of what she just checked out with. His comments were certainly rude; however, they were the simple blunt truth. Our parents managed to feed, dress and educate us, put a roof over our heads and pay for our medical care, didn't they? They managed by making sensible choices about what they could and could not afford and no one gave them a handout. We went to college and paid our own bills. We worked our way through. Mr. Obama and his ultra-liberal cronies not only want the taxpayers to fund what's currently on the table; they want to provide an even larger Federally funded banquet out of our tax dollars. There's only one problem. The number of taxpayers is dwindling. I remember being absolutely floored a few years ago when I discovered that fully 50% of the people in this country were being financially subsidized in one way or another by the Federal government. Now, with the severe economic downturn in this country, the problem is even worse. Not only is it worse, the system is ripe for plucking.

I recently hired an employee for part-time work. Within a few weeks, a full time position opened up and he was offered the job. Amazingly, he did not want full time employment because he didn't want to lose his unemployment checks! He simply didn't want to work for a living if he could avoid it. How many people remain unemployed in this country by choice because they have Federally funded benefits that allow them to do so? This employee is going to have a very short career with my company!

In a recent broadcast, the Fox News channel commentator Glenn Beck stated that only 42% of the employed in this country are working in the private business sector. The rest were connected to the government in one capacity or another. If you're pro socialism, that's great news, if you're pro free market economy you had better vote and make your voice heard. So what if you're only one tiny voice. Millions of voices speaking in unison can easily turn into one giant roar.

Most working class Americans are sick of paying to support other people's children. Why should they pay a penalty for someone else's unrestrained moment of passion when they're having enough problems trying to support their own families? There's a significant upsurge in the number of single females who give birth to "fatherless" children. It's not too difficult to figure out why. Children have become useful pawns in the "get it for free" game. It's economically advantageous to bear a child without the benefit of marriage. Then you can get it all. Your prenatal, delivery and medical care will be free; you will get housing, food, education and clothing; everything all handed out for free. The social stigma and financial burden have both been lifted from this event making it quite an attractive way of life to many.

One of my ambulance teams was dispatched to transport a 39 year old female in premature labor into a hospital with specialty care services for difficult childbirth situations. Her medical history was nothing short of amazing. She was single, unemployed and this was her thirteenth pregnancy. She had given birth to ten viable children and had one spontaneous abortion as well as another elective abortion in the past. During the transport, one of my nurses asked her why she continued to have so many children. Her answer was stunning. She told my nurse she would continue to have children as long as she was physically able to do so, because the more children she had, the more money she got from the State. She asked my nurse why she should go to work when she could make more money by having children and didn't need to pay for anything they needed.

In a similar situation, the sister-in-law of one of my employees is receiving all of the goodies our Public Aid entitlement programs offer. She is single with two children and lives with their father in a long term relationship. He is gainfully employed and has private healthcare insurance. Of course, as far as her official records are concerned, the father of her children is nowhere to be found. The family lives in reasonable comfort and is discussing the possibility of having another child since there would be no financial burden. In fact, there would be a financial gain. This is by far and above one of the most common abuses of the system. We transport the children of "single" mothers with Public Aid funding several times a day who nearly all claim that the fathers of their children are unknown. However, there is usually a second person to notify in the event of an emergency listed in their transfer records. That second person is most often an adult male with a different last name; however, his address and phone number is nearly always the same as the mother of the child.

This type of abuse happens on a daily basis. One such case recently came to light when the mother of a minor child landed in court for non payment of her ambulance transport bill. The mother was accompanied by her 14 year old son who had been a patient on board our ambulance as well as a male "friend of the family" who conveniently resided at the same address. The child had been taken to a local emergency room where he was examined and suspected of having meningitis. The hospital he was first taken to did not have pediatric intensive care services and our company was called to move the child into a hospital with more sophisticated resources. Meningitis is still a very serious illness and many children in this country still die from the effects of this disease. It was imperative that care be rendered to the child quickly. The transport was completed in good order. Fortunately, for this child, it was eventually determined that he did not have meningitis and he was discharged from the second hospital after a couple of days. We were not able to obtain any billing information at the time of transport so we attempted to obtain the information from the mother a few days later. She was uncooperative at best. She did not speak English so we had one of our Spanish speaking crew members talk to her. Multiple attempts were made in order to obtain information from the mother; all unsuccessful. Multiple bills were sent which were ignored. Eventually, the files went to our attorney for collection and the entire collection process was also unsuccessful. All attempts to communicate with the mother of the child were ignored. A law suit was filed and the mother was subpoenaed to show up in court for trial. The "friend of the family" accompanied the mother and stated that he was just a friend and was going to help the family out. It took more than half an hour to get this man to admit that he was the father of the child, that he was gainfully employed and had the means to pay for his sons medical bills. The Judge ordered him to pay for his son's care and he was given a monthly payment schedule. He immediately defaulted and my attorney has since placed a lean against his property. During the course of court proceedings, the mother of the child, through an interpreter kept insisting that she did not have to pay her bill. All of her friends told her that she didn't have to pay and nothing would happen if she didn't. This is not an extreme case. Unfortunately, it's quite commonplace.

Many people come to this country illegally and then give birth to a child on American soil. That child then becomes an American citizen based on rule of law. The law that allows this to happen was never intended to be used in such a manner. It was passed just after the Civil War in the late 1860's to ensure that the American born children of freed slaves whose parents were not born in this country were given their rights of citizenship. It was perhaps, one of the earliest civil rights acts in the nation and was both necessary and useful in its time. It's now useful as part of the reward system that entices illegal immigrants into this country. If the birth mother of a child is not in this country legally, why would anyone presume to think that the child she gives birth to is here legally either? It doesn't make sense. Dump the law.

Because of my position in the healthcare industry, I am a daily witness to the financial devastation that is being wrecked upon the taxpayers of this country by the presence of illegal immigrants on American soil. It's never ending and ever growing; it's an outrageous, illegal and expensive wrong being perpetrated against legal taxpaying residents. Get one thing straight here. I don't care what country they come from or what language they speak. This is not about race. It's about the law of the land and it's about the political leverage that our politicians hope to exert at election time by stirring up one ethnic group or another depending on what they wish to accomplish. You would think that members of these ethnic groups would catch on and stop allowing themselves to be emotionally triggered and used as pawns in such a degrading game. I, for one am not willing to foot the bill for this practice any longer. Illegal immigrants are a financial abomination that should not be tolerated. If they're not here legally then they should go back to the country of their origin and get in line to legally enter this country. If they are part of a seasonal migratory work group, they should be identified as such and enter this country in a legal manner. We should certainly be able to come up with an uncomplicated, secure process to allow these people to work legally in this country. This is a great nation and all who wish to come here and become productive members of society should most certainly be welcomed with open arms with one stipulation. They must enter this country legally and adhere to the immigration laws. If we stop handing out Public Aid entitlements to people who aren't in this country legally, they won't be quite so anxious to break our laws by crossing our boarders without proper registration. Just cut off the supply of free goodies. Cut off their subsidized way of life and many will voluntarily leave. There won't be any incentive to remain, in what to them is a foreign country. If they're not here legally, do not financially subsidize them out of Public Aid funding. If they end up in our hospitals, render humane, necessary care and then return them to the country of their origin.

Self Pay or Uninsured Patients:

The uninsured or **self pay** patient population is growing, becoming more numerous as more and more businesses cut back production teams or fail altogether and close their doors permanently. As unemployment rises, the number of uninsured patients also climbs. However, the bulk of the uninsured, or self pay patients are not the product of sudden or recent unemployment. A large number of these patients are from the shadowy underbelly of society; pimps, prostitutes, drug dealers, addicts, gang bangers and career criminals. These patients are easy to identify. Our ambulance crews know, as soon as they introduce themselves, speak with the patient and see their medical and demographic information that there's not going to be any pay source; that it's going to be a freebie. Most of these patient's are surprisingly up front about the fact that they're not going to pay for their medical care. We see to their need just the same.

In an emergent situation, care is always rendered, regardless of ability to pay and is identical to care that a patient with private insurance would receive. In an emergency, I have never seen or heard of a case where care was either altered or denied based upon the ability of a patient to pay for their care. Never trust a politician who tells you that hospital emergency rooms turn away uninsured patients, or that we refuse hospital admission if the patient does not have any financial means. While I suppose that the situation could potentially arise, in more than thirty years in the healthcare field, I have never seen or heard of a patient being turned away from a hospital or denied necessary care. In fact, the opposite is true. Not only is the patient admitted, the social services department immediately goes to work finding a pay source for the patient. If they do not qualify for Public Aid funding, they may well qualify for charity or foundation funds. In the event that no funding can be obtained, the patient may well experience financial obliteration until such time as they qualify for bankruptcy and Public Aid funding. That horrific and ugly event can and does happen; however, the medical care they urgently need is not denied by the hospital. Politicians who spew such nonsense, no matter how high up on the political food chain he or she may be are either woefully misinformed (which I doubt) or simply lying to gain impact in the political arena. It is quite true that a primary care physician may choose not see a patient in his office or agree to take the person on as a patient. A private physician has every right to do just that, however, when a patient enters through the emergency room doors of a hospital, they receive medical care. If they need to be admitted, they are. Period!

Another much larger group of self pay, or uninsured patients are in this country illegally. They are not turned away or denied medical treatment; care is faithfully rendered with no real expectation of payment. Very few of these patients give valid names, addresses, phone number or social security numbers and routinely claim not to be able to speak English. At times, they give fully false information that actually belongs to someone else; name, address, phone number and even Public Aid recipient numbers. It's not uncommon to have two or three interrelated families "share" their identities and use the same Public Aid numbers. The patience of healthcare providers is stretched extremely thin over this issue. More than anything, it's the deceit and lies that are the most difficult to tolerate. It's the theft of a costly product; healthcare that's most disturbing. No one likes to be taken advantage of; financially or otherwise. It's become more than tiresome. It's become financially devastating to healthcare providers and their practices and is part of what's causing a bitter racial divide and indiscriminant stereotyping which should not be happening in this country. Bitterness and resentment spills over onto people of the same or similar ethnic background who are in this country legally and are responsible, productive Americans. You can hang this one directly on the politicians. As long as the issue of immigration reform remains on the table as an unsolved problem in this country, the subject will continue to divide and plague us as a nation and politicians will continue to use it as a lever into office.

The last large group of self pay patients is simply not interested in purchasing healthcare insurance. They generally have the means to do so but choose to spend their money elsewhere. They tend to be younger without family obligations. They honestly do not feel they need to spend their money on insurance; believe that they are not going to become seriously ill or injured and probably have no idea what they will be financially faced with if they become medically compromised. While I wholeheartedly disagree with their take on this issue, I firmly believe that they have an inalienable right to make their own decisions in regard to this issue. Really, how dare the government of this country tell its citizens that they have to purchase a product? Many people site the legal mandate to purchase auto insurance and equate it with this subject. That argument doesn't work because driving an automobile is not mandatory. If you **choose** not to drive, you aren't mandated to purchase automobile insurance. Your right to make a free choice is still intact. There is no free choice connected to the healthcare insurance mandate that requires everyone to purchase insurance. The ensuing court battles over this issue will be very interesting to watch as they progress through the courts. On the other hand, anyone who can and does not purchase healthcare insurance by choice should clearly understand that I, as a healthcare provider am going to exercise all of my legal rights and pursue them for payment of their healthcare bills to the ends of the earth and beyond. They certainly shouldn't whine when they find out they are now going to be in debt for an extended period of time; sometimes years. I respect and support their right of free choice; however, they, in turn must respect my legal right to collect for my services and be willing to suffer the consequences of their own choices.

The reader should, by this time understand clearly that there is nothing wrong with the healthcare system per se. We don't have a healthcare crisis at all. What we have is a complete failure or crisis of **financial integrity** at all levels of the system. It's the management of the money, not the care that is at issue. The care is wonderful, the financial corruption rampant. The largest and most damaging financial crisis lies in the hands of the Federal government. Further interference by the Feds will only open up whole new avenues of opportunity to defraud the system. Most Americans already perceive the government to be corrupt and ineffectual and certainly don't want them involved any further in their healthcare. It's no quirk of fate that private insurance companies make money while the Federal government looses it when it comes to managing healthcare funds. The Federal sector of healthcare is far more corrupt and costly than the private sector because it is by far and above the easiest sector to rip off. So, it's simple. Privatize all healthcare.

Allow the private sector to compete for their market share of the product and get the federal government out of the insurance business altogether. Make certain that private sector abuse is so costly to the insurer that they cannot make a profit by engaging in it. Disallow PPO structuring and kickback arrangements between the insurers and providers so that the playing field is leveled and the patients are not manipulated and financially abused by kickback agreements. Get rid of entitlement funding waste for people who are not entitled. Stop giving it away recklessly and follow the successful example of privatized replacement policies for Medicare patients. If you look closely at what's going on in the financial arena of healthcare, it's obvious that the bulk of the corruption problems center around the government controlled sectors; not the private system. Quite frankly, if I were criminally inclined, I wouldn't have any problem at all coming up with a few schemes to defraud Medicare and Public Aid quite easily. On the other hand, coming up with a successful scam to defraud the private sector would be far more challenging. Get rid of what doesn't work and smooth out the wrinkles in what does.

Chapter 9

A Word To The Wise When Dealing With Your Healthcare Provider's Bills. We've Heard It All Already!

From a financial standpoint, healthcare is a strange product. It's the only consumer product that I know of where people believe they can consume and not pay for the service. Not only do they think they don't have to pay for it, they have no sense of immorality when they don't. It appears to be an accepted practice in a large portion of the population. If I provided the service and you don't pay for it, you've stolen it from me. Your argument is that you didn't know it was going to be so expensive. Well then, that's two of us. I didn't know it was going to be so expensive either.

Once the crisis of care is over, the patients and their families are faced with the daunting task of sorting out medical bills and statements which are confusing at best and often overwhelming. In most cases, families have no experience in dealing with the situation they're suddenly facing. They're usually exhausted and often emotionally distraught; at times, so stressed that they lash out in anger at the first opportunity. As a healthcare provider, I'm very much aware this is the case and dealing with such situations is a daily occurrence. Experienced personnel dealing with telephone calls are able to quickly determine the difference between an overwrought and frustrated caller compared to one who is intent on doing harm to the company if they don't get their way. Threats against the company are all too common. The following are examples of what we deal with on a daily basis and in some cases how the situation might have been improved upon with a sane, honest and rational approach to the problem.

Frustration and Anger:

We received a phone call from an irate patient who had just gotten her bill. The call was fielded by the general manager who was remarkably calm during the caller's long angry tirade. The patient ultimately informed our manager that she would not pay us one single penny. She was so irate over the poor coverage of her insurance policy that she was lashing out in anger at any target available. Eventually, the general manager managed to get a word in edgewise and told her we would work with her on the balance. He explained that part of the balance due was her deductible and would have to be paid. She was in no mood to be reasonable despite the fact that we were trying to work with her. She told us she would not pay us and hung up the phone. Five minutes later she called again and told the General Manager that she was very sorry and felt like a complete fool for having screamed and yelled at him when he was being very polite and trying to be helpful. Obviously, this was not a good way to open negotiations; however, at no time did she threaten or disparage the company, the service it provided or its employees. Her only attack was directed at the bill. She simply needed to vent. The General Manager explained that we would send an appeal to the insurance company on her behalf for further payment, and even if we did not receive any additional funds we would only hold her responsible for her deductible; at which time she burst into tears of gratitude.

Price Gauging:

All conversations with insurance companies between patients and providers alike, are recorded and become a part of the financial records file for any case in question. When we have a caller who states that the insurance company representative told them that we were price gauging, we're going to check on that conversation immediately. We call the insurance company, speak with a supervisor and have the conversation in question transcribed. If it turns out that the insurance representative did, in fact make such a statement, they just lost their job. In the ten years I have operated my present business, I've had countless people make such a statement. Only once was it true. The insurance company employee was immediately dismissed. No reasonably sane insurance customer service representative would make that statement because they are not allowed to do so according to the terms of their employment. It is a legal issue and no insurance company wants to be sued for interfering with a private business. Stop and think about it. Does anyone actually think, for one second that the customer service representative has any direct knowledge about the actual cost of providing any one single medical service? They process thousands upon thousands of charges on a daily basis. The most damning statement you might be able to get out of an insurance representative would be something to the effect of, "Yes, I see that it's expensive." and "no, I don't know why". After your successful heart transplant, would you call the surgeons office and say the same thing? If you make such a statement, you will be presumed to have a credibility issue. If, on the other hand, you state that you personally feel that we are price gauging, you are at least stating your own opinion which you are more than entitled to do. However, don't be surprised when we come right back at you with questions about your ability and background experience; training which would enable you to make that statement in an informed manner. Have you ever run a small business and are you involved in healthcare billing? Why don't you just ask us why the bill is so expensive? We will explain exactly what you were charged for and why it may not have been paid. We will also give you any information that we may have in our possession in order to enable you to get your insurance company to consider paying more for the services in question.

Everyone Should Just Accept What They're Paid and Not Bill The Patient:

Another transport, another phone call and an irate parent whose child had been emergently rushed into a level I pediatric trauma center with a skull fracture. This mother was objecting to the payment of her insurance policy deductible and copay assignment. Despite the fact that she understood quit clearly how her insurance policy was structured, she stated that her objection was based upon moral grounds. As far as she was concerned, patients should never be responsible for the payment of their medical expenses because they couldn't help it they needed the medical services. I fielded this one and asked her if she thought she shouldn't have to pay for food because she couldn't help it she had to eat. Her reply was that it wasn't the same thing at all because food was a product. I informed her that healthcare also was a product. Then I told her that she sounded pretty much like she was a left wing liberal democrat, which she confirmed. I told her unfortunately, I was a center right wing conservative so we would not be able to agree on this subject. However, I was willing to meet her in the middle and split her bill in half. She refused my generous offer, went to court and ended up paying the entire bill plus court costs. Personally held moral and ethical beliefs are trumped by rule of law every time.

Justifying Charges:

We are asked on a regular basis "How do you justify your charges?" My answer is invariably the same. I don't. I'm under no obligation to do so. I'm a private business entity that produces a product. Then, I go through my standard questions and ask if they have ever run a business or have healthcare billing experience; whether they have any direct knowledge about how to reduce my costs so that I might be able to bill less. I let them know that I would love to hear valid suggestions about how I might be able to do that. I usually ask the caller if they questioned the salesman about how they justified their charges when they purchased their last big screen HDTV. The correct question here would have been to ask me why it costs so much to provide this service. I would have gone to work and done my best to explain what each charge on the bill was for and why it cost so much money.

Talking With The Owner:

In many cases, when a caller doesn't hear what they want, they insist they be allowed to talk to the owner. The simple unvarnished truth here is the owner doesn't want to talk to them and probably won't. The owner is busy doing those things that owners do. He or she has already put qualified personnel in place to deal with your questions and problems. You might make it one step up the ladder to a supervisor, but you are not likely to get access to the owner on demand. The people you are talking to already have their marching orders from their boss so it's best to deal with them. You are not likely to get a different answer anyway. If you have a truly pressing issue which might alter the perception of your case, you don't need the owner. Talk it over with the billing representatives. They already know where their boundaries are. If your issue is compelling enough, they will bring it to the owner on your behalf.

I'm Being Taken Advantage Of:

We've had more than one patient's family member tell us we are sick and perverted because we're taking financial advantage of patients and their families while they're sick. I'm not sure exactly how that played out in the callers mind. I point out that we don't render care to well people; that all of our patients are sick and that the price structure is identical no matter what the diagnosis is. We don't charge on a graduated scale based on the severity of illness. One family member stated that our prices were exorbitant and that we purposely inflated the amount we charged to take advantage of people "when they are down and defenseless". This was not an argument worth having. The patient refused to pay despite the fact that she knew she would end up in front of a Judge. After the case was heard, the Judge peered over his spectacles at the defendant and said "Madam, they saved your child's life. Pay the bill". Is there a lesson here? If you decide to take your chances in court, don't count on sympathy to sway decisions your way. The legal system doesn't work that way. The Judge will base his findings on the rule of law. That's what Judges do. They interpret and apply laws.

The Patient Is Deceased:

At least once every week, we receive one or more of our invoices back in the mail with a copy of a death certificate enclosed and no payment. It then falls to us to explain that the bill still must be paid; that the patient was not deceased while in our care and that we put in a good deal of time and effort to make certain the patient arrived safely at the desired destination. We did our best to assure that nothing happened on our watch. We explain that we are still entitled to payment out of the proceeds of the patient's estate. Surviving spouses, parents or heirs must pay for the medical expenses regardless of the outcome. Explaining this is an unhappy task and is usually an uncomfortable event. The reality sometimes comes as a shock to elderly spouses to whom we are generally as helpful as is possible. There are some instances; however where sympathy rapidly dissipates.

We were called to transport a severely ill elderly woman from one hospital to another for a second opinion. The patient was receiving every conceivable form of life support and drug therapy available and was simply dying of multi organ failure at a rather advanced age. Her daughter still held out some hope for her mother's recovery and while we may feel that all hope is exhausted, we generally respect feelings to the contrary on the part of family members. However, we are very up front and honest about the situation when asked questions. The patient was a Public Aid recipient and this was going to be a very expensive trip. Public Aid, just like Medicare will not pay for a transport unless the receiving hospital is able to provide some service which the sending hospital can't. That was not the case in this instance. Both the sending and receiving hospitals were capable of the same level of care. The daughter was told that she would have to pay the bill and the reason was explained to her. She agreed and signed the appropriate papers. The transport, a very lengthy one requiring a full medical team was conducted safely and the patient was transferred without incident. We sent the daughter a bill and received a phone call a few days later. The daughter stated she was not going to pay the bill because her mother died. No sympathy here. This one will go to court. This was our mistake; we should have gotten cash up front before we did the transport. It's very common for Public Aid recipients to agree to pay for medical services which are not payable by the State in order to get what they want and then refuse to pay the provider.

Response To Threats:

Some people become extremely violent when faced with having to pay medical bills. While we understand that the anger probably goes much deeper than just one bill and we're most likely just the tip of the proverbial iceberg, if it's being taken out on us, we react very rapidly. In such cases, the entire account immediately goes directly to our attorney.

That anger can take different forms. Physical threats are rare, but do happen. One caller told my employee that she was going to come into our office and "take care" of him because he was a sick son of a bitch. Other threats pertain to activities that affect our business. When anyone threatens to report us to the Better Business Bureau, we inform them that we can no longer discuss the issue with them and our attorney will handle the case. The Better Business Bureau has no standing and is not able to intercede when a case becomes a legal issue. We have had two extreme cases where threats were made and carried out. In both cases, those threats were aimed specifically at interfering with our ability to conduct business. This is never a good idea. In fact, making good on such a threat can open up grounds for a lawsuit for damages against the person who has slandered the company or purposely attempted to cause them financial harm. If actual harm can be proven to have occurred and there is no proof that the company was actually guilty of any wrongdoing, the financial penalty can be extremely severe for those persons who carried out their threats.

In the first case, we had occasion to transport an executive who was administratively very high up in the American Hospital Association. He was quite wealthy and could certainly afford to pay his bills. However, he was accustomed to "courtesy" health care wherever he went because of his lofty position in the hospital association. Quite frankly, if I'm going to "courtesy out" a bill, it's going to be for someone in true need, not some guy living high off the hog in a wealthy suburb in the northwest Chicago metropolitan area with a summer home in one of the most exclusive areas of Florida. When he found out that we expected him to pay his bill, he blatantly told us that he would see to it that we never worked in three specific hospitals again because he golfed with the administrators of those facilities every week. Not being one to back down in a corrupt power play, I turned the account over to my attorney with every intention of proceeding through the collection process. My attorney was far more practical and explained that I was simply outgunned by wealth, power and high level corruption. I backed down, and regret it to this day. We lost the business in those three hospitals anyway and I've never given way in a similar situation since. If I had been able to obtain actual concrete proof that we lost business in those three hospitals due to his interference, I would have owned a nice summer home in Florida. I sincerely hope the administrator reads this book because I'm certain he will recognize himself as the corrupt, petty bully he is. The bill was a whopping $400.00. I believe he is retired in Florida as I write this.

The second case is of recent origin and is currently before the Office of the Inspector General under review. I could have simply let it go and eaten the unpaid balance, but it's just not in me to knuckle under when faced with threats. It's not the money. It's the bully tactics that set me off and trigger my stubborn resistance. We transported a patient who was critically ill and required an elevated level of care not available at the sending hospital. All went well with no unusual occurrences. We billed the insurance company who paid all but $900.00 and then sent a bill for the unpaid balance to the patient's home address. The patient's husband called and literally went ballistic over the fact that he had a remaining bill. He was loud, abusive and foul mouthed and said that the insurance company had paid enough and he was not going to pay any more. Despite his abusive behavior, we treated him exactly the same as any rational caller and offered to write off more than half of his bill and allow him to make interest free time payments for the remainder. He continued to scream filth and obscenities at us and told us that if we didn't write off his bill, he would contact newspapers, hospitals, the Better Business Bureau and that he would see to it that our business was ruined. We informed him that his case was being turned over to our attorney and gave him the information he would need in order to contact our legal firm if he so desired. He has attempted to make good on his threats. We were contacted by the Inspector General's Office with a request to provide all information concerning this transaction and are awaiting the results of their review. Whether or not we carry forward with this issue and pursue damages has yet to be decided. *(Update: As this book goes into print, the Inspector General's Office has informed us that they have advised the patient's husband to contact us to see if the discount we originally offered him was still on the table. It's not, and the case has been turned over to our attorney.)*

Billing For Services That Were Not Performed:

When patients receive bills from private ambulance carriers they understandably go into acute sticker shock. Their bills are far more expensive than local fire and rescue department bills and patients have no idea why. It's not at all uncommon for a patient or their family to assume that the private provider has billed for services they didn't receive. If a transport requires a full medical team, the cost can be truly mind boggling. The local fire department does a wonderful job with an initial rescue. It's what they were trained for and do everyday. Countless lives are saved through their dedicated service to their communities. They respond, stabilize and transport to the nearest hospital in an efficient manner. The hospital then begins the process of evaluation and treatment, taking the necessary steps to hopefully reverse the medical problem that brought the patient into their care setting.

When the hospital does not have sufficient resources to handle more complicated issues such as cardiac surgery, organ transplants or critically ill pediatric cases, they transfer the patient by private ambulance to a hospital with more sophisticated levels of care. All supportive care that has been initiated in the sending facility **must** be continued during the transport. If the supportive care is stopped, the patient will revert back to the original unstable state he or she was in when first admitted by the fire department. These cases regularly require additional equipment and medical personnel on board the ambulances. The fire department isn't set up to handle this type of problem. The vehicles used for these advanced care transports are set up in a highly sophisticated manner and the crew members have many years of specialized care experience. When these crews are very well trained with excellent experience, they make it look easy. It's not. It's difficult and expensive to provide this service. The more complicated the patient's medical problems are, the more costly it becomes to provide these services. Making it look easy is really not easy at all. The families of many patients look at a bill and can't understand why it's so expensive, after all, nothing untoward happened on the ambulance; it was all smooth sailing. Therefore they assume that we have billed for services that were not provided. If you're the one holding the bill, you're certainly entitled to a detailed accounting of the expenses that were billed. However, before you accuse your healthcare provider of fraudulent billing, you should discuss the issue with them in a rational open minded manner.

Making Up Events That Didn't Happen:

Healthcare is not perfect. Every patient is not going to survive and there's always going to be a margin of error to consider in the healthcare setting. That's not going to change. There's a human element to consider and humans sometimes make mistakes or errors in procedures or judgment. Healthcare providers are not without their fair share of day to day problems just like everyone else. They get tired, hungry, frustrated and angry, have problems with their home lives; go through divorces, births, deaths and financial disasters just like everyone else. It can, and sometimes does affect their ability to render care to a patient. Frankly, I think it's amazing that so many healthcare providers are able to put aside their personal lives and render faithful, dedicated care to you or your loved ones despite their own personal emotional obstacles. Once in a while, something does not go well, something is missed or miscalculated and there is a negative result because of it. Our courts are cluttered with such cases both real and perceived. Medical lawsuits are a booming business in this country and could easily be a subject for an entire standalone encyclopedia. Suffice it to say, for our purposes here, some cases are justified and some are not. Many of these cases are well publicized and a matter of public record.

One of the primary costs involved in providing healthcare services is the expense incurred for malpractice insurance. Fully 23% of our annual gross income is eaten up with insurance premium payments for one type of insurance or another. Think about that. Fully 23% of the bill we send to you is a result of this problem. Yes, we pass that expense on to you because it's part of our cost to do business. Anything that increases our costs increases the amount that I must collect to pay my employees salaries and other business expenses. Unfortunately, many lawsuits are either frivolous or based on something that never even happened. More than once, we've had someone try to "shake us down" over an event that never even occurred. They assumed we would allow our insurance company to settle for a modest sum of money rather than risk going into court. Both examples provided here were so totally ridiculous that we did neither. We didn't go to court and we didn't pay out any settlement money.

In the healthcare industry, a common cause for lawsuits are patients who have been dropped (in the care facility and in transit) during a difficult stage of movement from bed to chair or transport cot, cot to bed or while attempting to elevate the transport cot into proper position for movement to the ambulance. Loading and unloading the patient into and out of the back of an ambulance can also be very difficult, most especially if the patient is obese.

Transporting obese patients is quite common because obese patients have more medical problems than do people who are of average weight. We transported one such patient (460 pounds) from the hospital into an extended care facility. All went well despite the fact that it required two full teams to move her. The daughter of the patient was present during the transfer and commented on how kind and caring our crew members were. Everything changed when the daughter opened the bill for our services five weeks after the transfer had been completed. She called us and claimed that we had dropped her mother while loading her into the ambulance and since that time her mother had suffered medical problems as a result of our negligence. She made it very clear that she didn't really want to sue if it could be avoided because she knew her mother was difficult to move. However, she felt the least we should do was write off her mother's bill. We refused, held her responsible for the bill and told her to get an attorney. She paid the bill. We found out later she had used this same tactic on another ambulance company who simply wrote off her bill rather than deal with a legal mess.

A variation on the above theme resulted in the most bizarre, and I must admit, the most humorous allegation of abuse I've ever encountered. We had occasion, once again to move a very obese patient (560 pounds) from one hospital to another to obtain an elevated level of healthcare services. As in the last case, the patient's daughter was also present. After safely loading the patient into our ambulance with great difficulty and the assistance of two additional crew members as well as several helpful hospital employees, we were ready to proceed with the trip. Despite the fact that she had been told not to do it, the patient's daughter followed the ambulance because she was not familiar with the expressway route we had told her we were going to take. After the patient was safely delivered, the daughter thanked us for seeing to her mother's safe arrival. We proceeded with the standard billing process and the patient was left with a balance due for services not covered by her insurance company. Approximately six weeks later, the patient's daughter called and told us she was not going to pay the bill because we had seriously jeopardized her mother's life. I asked how we managed to do that and her response was so bizarre I couldn't possibly do anything but laugh. She informed me that as our ambulance was traveling down the expressway (at 65 miles per hour, no less), the back doors of the ambulance flew open, the cot became unlatched from its mooring and her mother flew out of the ambulance onto the expressway pavement. The mental picture this conjured up was just too immediately vivid for me to contain myself. I quickly placed my phone on mute and laughed quite uncontrollably. Once I stopped laughing and returned to the conversation, I asked the daughter how she could possibly know such a thing had happened. She said, she was following directly behind the ambulance in her automobile. I told her that if her story were true, she would have run her own mother over and our ambulance company would have made headline news all over the country. I told her to think up another more plausible story and in the meanwhile, pay the bill. She did; pay the bill that is.

I might as well throw in a little information about following ambulances while they are transporting patients. Never; never; never closely follow an ambulance in a private vehicle when they are in motion with their lights and sirens turned on. This is a suicidal activity. Your vehicle is much smaller than the ambulance and can not be clearly seen from all directions. The driver of the ambulance is released from certain "rules of the road" which you must still obey. If you don't know how to get to the destination hospital, the crew will usually give you directions so you can travel on your own in a safe manner. Your speeding presence behind the ambulance does no one any good and needlessly jeopardizes your own as well as other people's lives. No matter what happens, there is nothing you can do anyway so your reckless activity serves no positive purpose. When you arrive at the receiving hospital, you won't be able to remain with your family member anyway. You'll be placed in a waiting room while the receiving hospital admits your family member and gives urgent care. A member of the receiving hospital staff will eventually come get you when they've completed their initial assessment, rendered immediate care and settled the patient in.

One such occurrence resulted in our crew members calling the State police. Despite being told not to follow, one family member drove so recklessly that vehicles were forced to scatter all over the expressway. After a near disaster, which could have easily taken innocent lives, we called the State police from the ambulance and had the follower detained. Your speeding vehicle behind us only gives the driver of our vehicle one more thing to worry about. You're a distraction and hamper our progress. Your sense of urgency, which is certainly understandable, is no reason to place innocent bystanders at risk. No positive purpose is achieved by doing this. Give one of the crew members your cell phone number. They can contact you if necessary.

Transporting Your Family Member By Automobile:

What do you mean I have to pay this bill? This wasn't even an emergency! I could have taken my family member in the car! I didn't have any choice about who was called to transport my family member! I certainly would not have called your company; you're too expensive! No one on the ambulance even did anything! If the sending hospital couldn't take care of my family member, they should pay the bill! These are just a few of the outbursts we hear when families receive bills. It's all good until we get to the money part, then all hell breaks loose. So, let me answer quickly. Yes, you have to pay the bill; If it wasn't an emergency what are you doing in the emergency room; No you couldn't have driven the patient in the car; You didn't have a choice because the hospital must maintain the same level of care during transport that is being given in the ER and this was the only available company who could do it; If no one on the ambulance even did anything that's a good thing because all went as planned; No the sending facility is not going to pay your bill. There, now you understand why you have a bill and should pay it, right?

Let's just start with the basic premise that the patient is in the emergency room because something is wrong. If we can agree on that, we can move forward. Once the patient is admitted into the ER, medical contact and care has been initiated and it's not going to stop because a family member has changed their mind about the situation. The ER staff is legally obligated to take the case to completion. The primary purpose of the ER is to evaluate the situation, render stabilizing care, and enter the patient into the appropriate hospital care level for the specific problems that have been identified. If they can completely reverse the problem, you get to leave. If they stabilize the problem, but cannot reverse it you don't get to leave. An example of this would be a heart attack. The ER will give all appropriate medications to alleviate the symptoms and stop any further possible cardiac damage from occurring, but they do not fix the underlying problem that is causing the heart attack. Sure, the patient looks pretty good now. They're no longer sweaty, pale and in pain because the IV drugs we're giving them have gotten the situation under control and the patient is much more comfortable now. However, if we stop those drugs you're back to square one and the situation will most likely be worse the second time around. If the patient needs to be transferred, it must be done with all the same care the patient is currently receiving still in play. So NO! You can't stop the drugs and toss them in the car for a trip across town to another hospital that performs more sophisticated cardiac testing and/or surgery. All ambulance transports are not the same. A patient, who is having a heart attack, needs a sophisticated medical team that can provide the same level of service on board the ambulance the ER is providing. So NO! You were not allowed to price shop because these teams are not plentiful and you are lucky to get one quickly. Anything under an hour is fast. It is extremely expensive to hold a standby medical transport team at the ready just waiting for you to show up at the hospital in need of their services. Could you have used a less sophisticated and cheaper service? They could just yank the drug lines; toss the patient in the back of the ambulance and race against time to the other side of town, hoping that nothing goes wrong on the way. When it does, go wrong that is, you're going to sue the sending hospital and the ambulance company and you're going to win big time. The patient's medical problems need to remain stabilized and changes in condition addressed quickly in order to prevent further irreversible damage.

Back to the car situation; how were you planning on running your family members IV drugs during the automobile trip? That's going to take some really long extension cords. The medical team is trained to continue and adjust the patient's drug levels as needed during the trip. Any time the medical team is perceived as "not doing anything", that's a good thing. It means they were on top of their game and kept everything under control. Would you rather they just sit and wait for your family member to go into cardiac arrest so they can earn their pay by performing CPR on board the ambulance? Then would you feel better about that bill you received? At least the ambulance team will have done something you recognize as meaningful activity, right? And lastly, the sending hospital is not going to pay for your bill. If every single hospital out there provided the exact same services, the price of medical care would most likely quadruple. The hospital system is set up to make certain there are no large overlaps in care that would result in medical professionals sitting idle or worse yet, viciously competing for business. That waste of resources would cost a lot of money. Strategically placing medical services is simply good fiscal behavior. The physical location of hospitals, as well as the type of services they provide is carefully planned. The last thing you should think about; if you yank a family member out of a hospital AMA (against medical advice), your insurance company will not pay any bills. You will.

Last story; I promise. This is a tale of greed, avarice and deceit. A male patient in his 40's was taken to a local hospital emergency room with chest pain. His wife accompanied him. He was suspected of having an acute MI (heart attack) and all appropriate drugs were started via IV infusions with good results. His symptoms were relieved by the medications. The small hospital he was initially taken to did not have cardiology services; therefore, we were called to transport the patient to a more appropriate facility for advanced cardiac services. All IV drugs were continued during the transport which went quite well with the patient being admitted into the cardiac unit at the receiving hospital. We billed the insurance company for our services and eventually found out that the insurance check was sent to the patient and had been cashed by the patient's wife. The insurance reimbursement amounted to approximately 80% of the total charges. In cases such as this, if the patient or their family is up front and honest with us, we generally accept what the insurance company paid and write off the balance. When they're not honest, as in this case; we seek to recover the full cost of the transport. I am a firm believer that corrupt behavior should be given its just reward. We billed the patient through three cycles with no response until notice was sent that the bill was slated to go into collection. Obviously, the patient's wife had every intention of keeping the funds at our expense. Once she realized that we were going to pursue legal action, the patient's wife sent a check (for the full amount of the bill) and sent the following letter.

"Let me just say that I find this bill ridiculous. We were at hospital X and because cardiology is limited there, we were transported to hospital Y. If hospital X isn't equipped for the test my husband needed, it's their responsibility to pay for its patients to be taken elsewhere. Also, at the time of transport, there was absolutely no emergency. I could have easily driven my husband but that request was denied. This is precisely the reason our country is in the fix that it's in. re; health care---GREED!"

My, my, such righteous anger! The check she sent was embellished with a biblical scripture. Oh, and by the way; the patient's wife had no idea that we were aware she had received payment from the insurance company and had cashed the check with the intent of defrauding us for her own gain. The insurance company is required to give the provider of service that information upon request. We're in agreement with the patient's wife about one thing. Healthcare is definitely in trouble and she's spot on. It's all about greed and hers is a classic example of just that.

Chapter 10

A Few Interesting Tidbits. Definitely Worth Perusing! Questions, Answers and Dissertations.

Why is there such a push going on to place all medical records into computerized systems?

First of all, every single person who's ever consumed any healthcare services in the past needs to clearly understand that records for their care belong to them; not the doctor, hospital or other care giver. Those records are simply stored by the healthcare provider. You'll have to pay to get copies in most cases; however, you can most certainly access them at will and in theory, you should have some say about how those records are handled and distributed. Additionally, the only people who are legally allowed to see your records are healthcare providers directly involved with your care. Anyone else who wishes to view your records must have a signed authorization from you or your power of attorney. In other words, your records are private.

We come to a dilemma about your records when we're required to transfer them electronically to someone else. Does that "someone else" have the legal right to see your records?

Storing records electronically **on site** at your doctor's office, the hospital or other medical facility makes sense. This is probably a good thing.

They can be called up and printed out very quickly for review purposes and take up very little physical space. Consider the amount of paper being stored in this country in the form of medical records as you read this. It's a miracle that anyone ever finds your files. However, the proposal that records be electronically transferred from their original site to another location presents issues of confidentiality. During the transfer process, those records are vulnerable to invasion. I have yet to see a computer program or system that cannot be breached by a hacker once it's become accessible online. Wherever there's a person smart enough to create a secure system, there's always someone else a little smarter who's able to invade it.

The Obama administration cites an improvement in the quality of care and a reduction in medical errors as reasons to mandate this activity. They could have used better arguments. The quality of healthcare will remain exactly as it is. It's human activity in the care setting that defines quality in healthcare, not record keeping. The reduction in medical errors is based on the assumption that no one will make errors when inputting information into the computers. Back to garbage in, garbage out. Errors will continue to occur whether records are written or typed. Typing is just easier to read, errors and all.

The conversion to electronic record keeping is not cheap; quite the opposite. Each of my ambulances will require an investment of nearly $6000.00 to start this system up, and will then cost me an additional $600.00 each on an annual basis in order to maintain my "subscription" to the provider of the software. This is a per ambulance fee. I must also pay for and maintain a system in my office to collect this data and then transfer it to another site. This cost, of course will be transferred to the patients in the form of higher bills. The transferred data will be used to generate State mandated reports by my EMS (Emergency Medical Services) system hospital and those records contain your name and other personal information. I have no control over the confidentiality of those records once they leave my office. How long will it be before the Feds mandate the transfer of your medical information into their possession?

I don't think this conversion to electronic data storage and transfer has anything to do with quality of care or error avoidance at all. What it will do is something entirely different. It will supply statistical data to any and all comers who may or may not be authorized to peruse your medical records. The question of who is authorized to view your records or the data generated from them is at issue here. Once this system is in place; the person charting or creating your records, for the most part will "click" standardized, preset boxes to record vast amounts of data in a robotic precision-like manner. That data can then be collected, transferred electronically into a central collection area and used to generate nationwide statistical data; statistics which can then be used to manipulate the availability of healthcare to certain patient populations. Reimbursement for medical services might then be predicated upon cost benefit criteria. For example; if you're 65 years old, you might not be allowed to have a liver transplant, whereas the 35 year old drug addict might get one instead. Statistically, the addict would have a longer life span and might eventually be more productive. Perhaps I'm too suspicious of the Federal government; however, I don't like the idea that my personal records will soon be flying around in cyberspace for anyone to grab. You be the judge. They are, after all your records.

What's tort reform?

Tort law deals with the legal rights of any person who has suffered physical, emotional and/or financial injury at the hands of another. It's the law under which medical malpractice lawsuits fall. In this country, lawsuits for malpractice, real and perceived are a booming industry with virtually no limits on what damages may be assigned to the plaintiff if they win and how much attorneys may charge for their legal services. This leads to extremely high malpractice insurance costs for healthcare providers and the practice of defensive medicine in order to avoid being sued. These costs are not absorbed by the healthcare providers alone. They cost the entire nation one way or another. Much of that cost is spread out amongst the patient population. If you remember, previously I told you that about 23% of my company's income was spent on one type of insurance or another and the cost was passed on to the consumer. The next time you receive a bill for healthcare services; remember, roughly one quarter of the money you're paying goes toward your healthcare provider's insurance costs. Additionally, defensive medical practices cost the healthcare insurance companies and patients enormous sums of money.

Tort reform advocates seek to limit, through federal law, frivolous lawsuits, restrict the amount attorneys may charge for their services and place a cap on the maximum amount of money that may be awarded to a plaintiff for damages. Some individual States have already enacted their own laws with appreciable results. Mr. Obama seems to be resistant to the idea of reforming this system, despite its negative impact on the cost of healthcare. Is he planning to take up a career in medical malpractice law when his presidency is at an end? Tort reform would certainly decrease the need for malpractice lawyers.

Who is the American Medical Association and what do they do?

The America Medical Association, or AMA is a voluntarily joined organization of doctors. They have a somewhat checkered history which can be accessed through the internet by typing "Wickipedia American Medical Association" in your browser bar. Formed in 1847, they are headquartered in Chicago, Illinois. At one time, they enjoyed extensive membership; however, over the years their membership and impact on the medical community have dwindled sharply. One of their most lucrative tasks is the coding initiative that all healthcare providers must use when billing medical claims. This system looks a lot like the Dewey decimal system used in libraries across the country. The AMA produces these codes at the request of the Federal government (for which they receive handsome financial rewards out of taxpayer money) and then sells these codes in book and CD form throughout the medical community. No healthcare provider is able to bill without current codes produced by this association. It's a nice lucrative gig.

Who is CMS and what do they do?

CMS, or The Center for Medicare and Medicaid Services is a Federal governing and oversight body which is controlled by the Department of Health and Human Services. The current secretary of this department is Kathleen Sebelius who was appointed by Mr. Obama. Amongst other things, CMS is responsible for the production and revisions of the Federal Register contents which apply to healthcare. The Federal

Register lists all laws affecting the county, not just healthcare matters. Healthcare, of course is an important part of the document and the register outlines, word for word exactly what medical care and equipment will or will not be reimbursed to providers for Medicare and Medicaid recipient services. This is complete government control over payment issues in the Federally funded medical community. CMS can and does decide, at any time not to fund certain types of medical procedures and equipment to recipients of Medicare and Medicaid. Healthcare issues are reviewed and revised at a minimum, on an annual basis and then submitted to congress to be passed into law. It is a huge and cumbersome document which I am quite certain no one in congress has ever read. It's up to the healthcare provider to know exactly what's in that part of the document which pertains to them and adhere to it without exception. CMS does not pay your medical bills. Its function is to oversee the specific details of your care and make certain that your healthcare providers are adhering to the law, most especially when it comes to issues related to billing the federal government for services provided to the consumer.

CMS is responsible for the oversight of the insurance companies that handle the federal government's insurance programs. They are supposed to make certain that waste, corruption and abuse are not being engaged in.

How much money does the average person pay into Social Security and Medicare in their lifetime?

There is no actual average. The total amount you've paid into the system is completely dependent upon how much your salary is and has been in the past. However, you can find out your own numbers quite easily. Each year, the Social Security Administration sends you a report reflecting the status of your "account" with the Federal government. The next time you receive one of those reports, instead of tossing it aside as irrelevant, take a close look at what you've paid in and think about that number. During my lifetime, despite the fact that I've never broken employment since the age of 16, I still don't have a great deal of money paid into the system. Despite the large bite the Federal government takes out of your paycheck, remarkably little of it goes into your Social Security and Medicare Funding. Your individual report will tell you exactly how much money both you and your employer have paid into Social Security and Medicare. What I find the most shocking in my own report is the amount of money paid into Medicare. There hasn't been enough money paid into the system for me to spend even one week in a hospital with a serious illness. There simply isn't enough money allocated to Medicare and Social Security out of your tax dollars to take care of all of the incoming expenses. The Feds want to raise the amounts we pay in taxes to cover the shortfall for both Social Security and Medicare. Given that they've raided these funds in the past to cover other government expenses, I don't think I like that idea. A raise in this tax rate would negatively impact the business sector of the nation's economy as well as the ordinary citizens of this country. Not only is the employee taxed for these items, the employer must match that same amount paid by their employees. The expense of doing business will, once again rise and the increase will be passed along to the consumers in the form of higher prices for goods and service. Healthcare is certainly not going to be exempt. It would make far more sense for the Feds to cut out their wasteful spending and allocate more of our current payroll tax money into the Medicare and Medicaid system. We need to fund less government waste and more Social Security and Medicare services. I'd have no problem paying a higher percentage for these services as long as the Feds reduced the Federal tax burden by the same percentage. Let's just shift the allocation of our tax dollars and send people to Washington DC who understand the meaning of the term fiscally responsible.

Keep your reports from year to year and compare the projected amount of money you'll receive from Social Security every month after you reach retirement age. Don't expect to see any significant amounts. If you're depending solely upon the Federal government for your retirement income, you may well have to exist at below poverty level. Take those numbers seriously and make wise financial decisions while you're young enough to impact your own financial wellbeing during your retirement years. If you're relying upon the Feds to take care of you in your senior years, you're going to be sadly disappointed; in fact, you're going to be destitute.

What's all this talk about eliminating the IRS and revamping the Federal tax system? What's a VAT?

As soon as someone mentions the IRS, nearly everyone has a negative feeling descend upon them. Just the mention of this agency by name can quite literally ruin their day. The Internal Revenue Service is not popular. Beyond not being popular, it's an expensive and cumbersome system to maintain and run. No one likes the IRS and virtually everyone, except people employed by them, would prefer to see it become extinct. It's an archaic, expensive system and needs to be eliminated. Soon!

The most popular replacement suggestion, at this point in time is an end user tax. We'd all see a huge hit when we went out to shop, that's for sure; but think about it for a minute. Most people in this country, **who pay taxes** forfeit between 30% and 60% of their earned salaries to their city, State and Federal taxing agencies. What if their payroll checks reflected the actual amount of money they earned? What if they didn't have to sweat through income tax preparations? Wouldn't that be a wonderful thing? Instead of taking home $1500.00 per week, they would take home between $2000.00 and $3000.00, depending upon what tax bracket they currently fall into. They can choose to spend or not, as the case may be. Spend and you pay taxes. Save and you don't. As a saver, that sounds very attractive to me. I'm tired of being taxed when I earn and then taxed again when I receive interest.

The current system is set up in an uneven manner to tax people who are responsible enough to report their taxes correctly and pay what the Feds consider to be their just due. There are a huge number of people who either underpay or pay nothing at all into the system. I, for one would like them to pay their fair share. I would like to see every single person who resides in this country pay into the system. If employers paid everyone who works for them the full sum of their earnings and then taxed them when they purchased goods and services, it would insure that everyone contributes to the support of this country. It would certainly level the playing field.

How would it work? Let's say that the Federal tax rate was set at 25%. When you go out and spend $10.00 on tomato plants for your garden, you will pay an additional $2.50 for your fair share of Federal taxes.

If a corporate executive purchases a new yacht for $10,000,000.00 he would pay the same tax percentage and not be able to write his purchase off as a business expense either. His tax would amount to $2,500,000.00. I like that and so should every working, tax paying person in this country. You say you want to tax the rich? This system would eliminate inequitable tax breaks for everyone. Little spending; little taxes. Big spending; big taxes.

Another enormous benefit would be the taxation of everyone who works "off the books" for cash. It wouldn't matter if they were working for cash or not because when they spend that money, they pay their fair share. Just think about that. We'd be taxing pimps, prostitutes and drug dealers. The next time you see a pimp driving a Rolls Royce, think about it. There'd be no more manipulative tax breaks for anyone in the high income brackets in this country. So what if corporations no longer pay taxes or their tax rate is minimal with no corporate dodges built in to the system? Their wealthy executives, who are recipients of the company profits, will pay taxes when they buy their huge estates. We could simply tax "out of country" purchases as well, so that villa in the south of France will still net income for the American economy. Most corporations would immediately increase their business ventures, hire new employees and give raises. It's what businesses do in order to compete when left with enough funds to do so. All that money would end up in the hands of consumers who would purchase more goods and services and support the economy. Businesses would swarm back into this country from overseas to such an extent that the government would be able to pick and choose the nature and number of the businesses allowed to produce in this country. Better secure those borders first, though!

By and large, middle class Americans support a system similar to this because they're the ones who are paying taxes in this country. On the other hand, those people who don't pay taxes do not want to see this type of reform put into practice for obvious reasons. They love their free candy. They have no desire to help support the system.

Can there be adjustments? Sure! It's easy. You can exempt certain types of staple foods in the grocery store using bar codes; tax high end luxury items and junk food at the full tax rate. Hamburger, no tax; lobster tail full tax. Similarly, an exemption could be made available for the first $35.000.00 paid for an automobile to include two vehicles, or the first $500,000.00 paid for a home to include two homes. There are any number of ways to exempt certain purchases for ordinary, necessary expenses so our low income folks are not unduly penalized. We could establish a fair share tax and still achieve taxation equality with a system such as this.

I firmly believe that a tax system set up in a similar manner would net the Federal government far more income than it enjoys at present and eliminate the stranglehold that the IRS has on the taxpaying American public. We could eliminate the actual cost of funding the IRS and the enormous archaic tax code system it pretends to enforce. However, no system such as this should be put into play unless the Federal government **completely dismantles** the current system and abolishes the payroll taxes we now pay. Otherwise, we will become saddled with the same system presently in play in the socialized countries of the world. If the Feds keep the current system and then initiate an end user tax such as the one described above, we would have what is commonly referred to as a VAT or value added tax. Pure European socialism at its worst! There are rumors that Nancy and Harry are pushing for this and Mr. Obama is not taking the idea off the table. If this country establishes a VAT, it will go the same way it's gone in European countries; ever spiraling upward.

Redistribution of wealth – What is it?

Every single working American who pays Federal and State taxes is affected by the redistribution of wealth that takes place in this country. For instance, Medicare is a redistribution of wealth. Your taxes are funding healthcare for the elderly in this country. Public Aid assistance is also a redistribution of wealth and funded by both State and Federal taxes. A very large number of working Americans want to see reasonable limits set on who can receive assistance and how much they should be allowed to receive. I believe that most taxpaying Americans do not object to a certain amount of redistribution. We certainly wouldn't want to see an elderly senior neighbor starve to death before our very eyes. However, there are limits to what most people feel the government has a right to mandate; to take away from one person and give to another. During the most recent Presidential campaign, "Joe the Plumber" outed Mr. Obama on this issue and made it into the National news for weeks. The American public was so starry eyed with awe at the social concept of electing Mr. Obama it chose not to heed an abundantly clear warning. Next time, pay attention to what's being said, not who's saying it. I wonder how much Mr. Obama is willing to reduce his gross income in order to support entitlement programs. I wonder if he's willing to redistribute his wealth down to my financial level in order to adhere to his own liberal philosophy.

What's an unfunded mandate?

Most of our State Governors are hopping up and down yelling "no more unfunded mandates". These mandates are being imposed on the States by the passage of Federal laws. There's only one problem. These laws require large sums of money to implement and the States don't have it. Most States believe that Washington should put their money where their mouth is; literally. However, the Feds don't have the money either. Listen up folks. This country is broke. The goose is no longer laying golden eggs, so all of you out there who've skated by without contributing to the system had better get ready to pony up! Obamacare directs the States to provide increased healthcare initiatives; however there isn't any way to fund them. In fact, in some instances, such as Public Aid initiatives, if the State does not provide those Federally mandated services, they'll loose what little funding they currently have. Unfunded mandates are already overburdening State budgets throughout the country. We really don't need anymore. We really need a whole lot less.

How to contact your politicians and why you should do so.

Most people in this country have no idea just how easy it is to contact their State and Federal senators and representatives. Even if they know how to get it done, they're intimidated by the title of the office. No one should ever be shy about telling their congressmen and women what they think or want. You elected them and they work for you. Never forget that government is "of the people, by the people and for the people" and you are their employers. You are "the people"! If they can't or won't do the job you hired them for, you can fire them. If you want to be effective when contacting your politicians, be polite. Firm and to the point is fine; just don't be rude. Rude and aggressive language only serves to diminish you and your message. The more rational and well thought out your correspondence or telephone call is, the more likely you are to be taken seriously.

If you want to contact your congressman by email, simply type "email senator John Doe" or whatever your representative's name is in your internet browser bar. You should be able to access their State web site quite easily. At that point, you can either write down the telephone numbers for their offices and call them, or click on the "contact me" button in their web site to send an email. If you call their office you can leave a message asking for a return call. Some will answer you and some will not. As long as you state a legitimate reason for your call, you should be able to speak with a human being. Much of the time, you will be able to express an opinion on any given political subject which will be passed on to your representative. It's not uncommon for me to receive a phone call back from a senator or representative when I have a specific question about pending legislation which might affect small businesses. Give it a try. It's your country and you have every right to speak your piece. Unlike healthcare, speaking your piece, making your opinion known is one of your inalienable rights.

Bibliography

Supporting Documents

All **financial information** and statistical data was provided by the privately held corporation owned and operated by the author. That data is not available to the general public and is restricted from release by the Health Insurance Portability and Accountability Act under statutes passed into law by the Federal government.

All specific **patient case studies** were provided by the privately held corporation owned and operated by the author. That data is not available to the general public and is restricted from release by the Health Insurance Portability and Accountability Act under statutes passed into law by the Federal government.

All **statistical data** was provided by the privately held corporation owned and operated by the author. That data is not available to the general public and is restricted from release by the Health Insurance Portability and Accountability Act under statutes passed into law by the Federal government.

Doctors Hospital Medicare and Medicaid Scandal:

"Historic Doctors Hospital slated for auction"

Published in the "Chicago Maroon" By Nancy Lo, June 2nd, 2005

http://www.chicagomaroon.com/2005/6/2/historic-doctors-hospital-slated-for-auction

Psychiatric Outpatient Medicare and Medicaid Scandal:

"Psyched: Nursing Home Patients Cheated Out Of Care"

CBS channel 2 News CHICAGO by Pam Zekman, Feb 28, 2007

http://cbs2chicago.com/investigations/2.investigators.equip.2.335523.html

Humana Class Action Lawsuits:

1. Humana Settles Class-Action Suit With Physicians -- AAFP News Now ...Oct 21, 2005 ... Health insurance company Humana has settled its class action lawsuit with family physicians. www.aafp.org › ... › AAFP News Now Archived Stories - Cached - Similar
2. Managed Care Challenged in Class Action Lawsuit Sep 29, 1999 ... The Humana lawsuit is brought by five individuals on behalf of themselves ... class action had been filed against Aetna on October 4, 1999. ... library.findlaw.com/1999/Oct/1/126766.html - Cached - Similar
3. Humana to pay $2.8 million settlement in insurance class action ...Mar 20, 2008 ... Kansas City, KS: (Mar-19-08) A class action lawsuit was brought against Humana Inc. and other insurers, alleging that the companies engaged ... www.lawyersandsettlements.com › Settlements - Cached
4. Class Action Lawsuits Filed Against Humana, Others | Franklin Gray ...Humana announced that they have been named as a defendant in two separate class action lawsuits. In a class action lawsuit filled in the United States www.franklingrayandwhite.com/.../class-action-lawsuits-filed-against-humana-others.cfm - Cached - Similar

United Healthcare, Cigna & Aetna Class Action Lawsuit:

1. UnitedHealthcare: Out-of-network ASCs file class action over low ...May 17, 2010 ... HLB originally filed a class-action lawsuit in 2009 alleging that ... more clear now that United did not appropriately calculate UCR rates. ... www.fiercehealthpayer.com/.../unitedhealthcare-out.../2010-05-17 - Cached

2. MSSNY - United Healthcare Settlement This suit, which was filed on March 15, 2000, alleges that UHC's subsidiary, Ingenix Corp., developed a database to determine UCR, but the database was ... www.mssny.org/mssnyip.cfm?c=i&nm=United_Healthcare...

www.ingramcontent.com/pod-product-compliance
Lightning Source LLC
Chambersburg PA
CBHW021944170526
45157CB00003B/919

* 9 7 8 1 4 5 0 2 5 6 3 5 3 *